CONFESSIONS
OF A
SLOT MACHINE
QUEEN

A MEMOIR

Permission requests should be mailed to EugeniaBooks, P. O. Box 5565,
Madison, Wisconsin, 53705.

Certain names in this book have been changed for reasons of privacy.

Library of Congress Control Number: 2009937457

Adell, Sandra.

Confessions of a Slot Machine Queen: A Memoir/ Sandra Adell.—1st edition

ISBN 978-0-9842671-0-1

1. Adell, Sandra—Family. 2. Gambling addictions. 3. Casino gambling—
Economic and sociological impacts. 4. Black women writers—Autobiography
and memoir.

Published in the United States of America by EugeniaBooks, Madison,
Wisconsin

www.EugeniaBooks.com

First Edition, 2010

Designed by James Arneson
Edited by Polly Kummel

Printed in the United States of American on acid-free paper

CONFESSIONS

OF A
SLOT MACHINE
QUEEN

A MEMOIR

SANDRA ADELL

May the Spirits of My Ancestors Be My Guide

To Andrew:
Sylvia's mother says,
Stay true to yourself and
follow your dreams.
            Sincerely,
            Sandra Adell
            June 4, 2010

Canewell: Do you gamble?
            I'm looking for a gambling
            woman.
Ruby: Ain't nobody gonna do no gambling.
            You have to gamble by yourself.

—August Wilson, *Seven Guitars*

No more text sex mess
No more zoot-suit mayors
shuffling skeletons and abuses
like gamblers losing pay checks
in motor city casinos.
No more boarded-up windows,
No more broken trees,
or dilapidated buildings
where junkies, rodents
and vermin spring.
We want our city back.

—Melba Joyce Boyd,
"We Want Our City Back"

CONTENTS

PROLOGUE

"I'll take that in ten hundred-dollar bills," I said as I handed my voucher to the man behind the cashier's counter. The Queen had done it again! I hadn't been in the casino more than thirty minutes and had won $1,011 on a ten-times-pay machine. The cashier counted out ten crisp hundred-dollar bills, one ten, and a single. I stuffed the single and some change from my pocket in his tip box and neatly folded the hundreds in a little leather wallet I used to keep my gambling money separate from my real money. I always left a small tip for the cashiers whenever I won $1,000 or more. It was my way of keeping my mojo going, of feeding whatever goddess was blessing me with good luck so she would keep on sending little stacks of hundred-dollar bills my way. As I put my money away, a voice in my head whispered, "You need to leave. Right now. You got what you came for. You have bills to pay. *Leave.*"

But I was on a roll. Not exactly what high rollers would consider a roll, but for most ordinary slot players $1,000 ain't nothing to sneeze at. I had brought $500 with me on this trip, money I could've used for something practical, like paying the plumbing bill that had arrived in that day's mail. Instead, I decided to try my luck just one more time before bringing this adventure in Casinoland to an end once and for all. I had tried it before, after I won $6,000 for the second time at Ho Chunk Casino, the place where this whole thing started, in Wisconsin, about forty-five miles from my home in Madison. But the lure of the slots was too powerful. This time a $200 wager had brought me $1,011, so now I could gamble with the remaining $300 and still come out ahead.

"*Leave now,*" the little voice kept whispering. "*Don't give the money back.*" I ignored it and proceeded to lose all of it—$1,300. It didn't make sense! Even as I pulled the hundred-dollar bills out of my wallet and stuck them in the machines, I kept asking myself, "What the hell are you doing?" But the machines kept beckoning, blinking their lights, calling out to all the slot junkies wandering around like zombies as they looked for the "right one" to feed. I felt sick as I pulled bill after bill out of my wallet and stuck them in one machine after another. They were greedy, especially the Jeopardy machine, which made an irritating slurping sound every time I hit the Bet Max button.

By the time I was down to my last two hundred-dollar bills, my hands were shaking. I had started sweating but blamed it on a sudden hot flash. My stomach ached from tension. My physical reactions were warning me that I was engaging in a dangerous activity. But I kept right on giving the money back and pretending it didn't matter. Pretending there was plenty more where that came from. As I wandered through the casino toward the exit pretending not to have a care in the world, a slot attendant greeted me as I passed her. "You look very pretty tonight. I noticed you when you walked in. I hope you're having some luck." I put on my diva smile and thanked her. I wasn't surprised that she had noticed me when I made my entrance. I was one of only a handful of black people in the casino that night: a middle-aged black woman clad in black, expensive gold jewelry gleaming in the artificial light. Yeah, I stood out. I just hoped my stride wouldn't betray the weakness I felt in my legs as I made my way through the exit.

As I drove home I vowed, once again, to stop this charade, to lay down my crown before it was too late. It was taking too much energy to preside over this bizarre fairyland, even in my imagination. This was it. I was never going back.

I crawled into my bed exhausted, my mind drifting back to a spring afternoon when I had decided to do something really out of the ordinary and went gambling. I got lucky that day, and suddenly my orderly existence turned into a private hell. After tossing and turning and sighing to myself for I don't know how long, I feel asleep. The slurping sounds and blinking lights of the Jeopardy machines invaded my dreams.

PART ONE

CHAPTER 1

Ho Chunk

Bewildering. That's the only way to describe my behavior after a trip to Ho Chunk Casino in the spring of 2005 brought me a quick $1,100 win. Before I realized what was happening, I had gone from having no interest in casinos and gambling to thinking about nothing else. In fact, the few times I had been in casinos before April 30, 2005, I found them nauseating. Too much noise, too many gaudy lights, too much smoke, and too many people engaging in what I thought was a really stupid activity—putting money into machines and watching the reels spin round and round. And the people seemed to have the same strained look on their faces, as if their lives depended on the outcome of those spinning reels. So when my friend Bev called that day and invited me to go to Ho Chunk with her, I told her what I usually told people who asked me to go gambling with them: "No. I don't like casinos. I even went to Monte Carlo, and that's supposed to be the most famous casino in the world and didn't like it, so I'm not about to go to *that* place."

This time all I got out was, "No, I don't like casinos," before I heard myself saying, "You know what? Yeah. Come and pick me up. Let's go."

Bev had caught me at a vulnerable moment. For months I had been dealing with the death of a long relationship. It had not been easy. There were days when I felt listless, when all the things I once found emotionally and intellectually fulfilling—teaching, writing, working out, sailing and wind surfing on Lake Mendota—were not enough to ease the pain of losing the man I had deceived myself into believing was some kind of poetic genius. He was hateful. For years I put up with his hatefulness in exchange for the increasingly rare moments when he was charming, kind, witty, and stimulating, both intellectually and sexually. We parted in August 2004. Now, nine months later, I was still trying to clean up the emotional wreckage I had become, a result not only of the breakup but also of looking deeper into myself than I had ever dared to do before. Teaching helped. I also managed to fill up two or three evenings a week with various academic and artistic committee meetings. But the semester would end in two weeks and I was worried. What then?

When the poet left, he took his share of the household income. Although he told me to call if I needed anything, I wasn't about to let him know that my financial situation was tight. I told him that I'd get along just fine. But I hadn't saved enough from the nine-month salary I'm paid as a university professor to get through the summer. My second stream of income, from acting and commercial print modeling jobs, had dwindled to a trickle, the result of advertisers tightening their budgets and celebrities taking over the commercials market. Not to mention that I'm *une femme d'une certaine age*, that is, middle aged. And a black woman. My demographic wasn't exactly going to bring in big bucks for hungry advertisers seeking new ways to place their clients' products. That's why I agreed to go to Ho Chunk that Saturday afternoon. I needed my friend's company to help me pull out of a deep and funky mood. Another reason was that this excursion offered a brief escape from the world of academia, a world into which I never quite fit. After more than twenty years at the University of Wisconsin–Madison, first as a graduate student in the Department of Comparative Literature and then as a professor in Afro-American Studies, I was tired of trying to live up to other people's images of a black woman in academe.

Bev instructed me to bring along at least $300 in cash. She also told me how to dress. "Now don't go gettin' all dressed up," she said. "You don't want to be conspicuous 'cause people might be looking. Don't bring a big purse, just something to put your money in. And be careful how you pull it out. You don't want people seeing how much money you got." I did as my gambling mentor told me. I put on a pair of jeans, a Bucky Badger T-shirt, and a blue baseball cap. And I withdrew $200 from the bank and stuffed it into my fanny pack, along with my driver's license.

I thought $300 was a bit too much to lose. I'd been on a tight budget for months, tracking every cent I spent, and allowed myself only $200 a month for nonessential expenses such as movies, theater and concert tickets, and the wines I love to drink. I rode the bus to work to save money on gas and parking. I washed my car myself. I'd stopped eating out. I did not shop. I even gave up the five-dollar bags of popcorn mixed with caramel crisps from Garrett's Popcorn Shop that I used to treat myself to whenever I was in Chicago. "You can't afford to spend five dollars on a little bag of popcorn," I'd tell myself as I rushed to an audition or a commercial print "look-see." I needed to save money.

Now I was getting ready to throw away my pocket money for the entire month of May in one day. But it was worth it if it would keep my demons at bay for a while longer. Plus, I'd be leaving my money with the Ho Chunk Nation where some of it might trickle down and do distant kin some good. Like many African Americans, I have a great-great-grandmother on my mother's side who was Native American and from whom I apparently inherited not only a look but an affinity for Native people.

◆ ◆ ◆

Bev and I left for Ho Chunk around two in the afternoon. We drove west along Highway 12 through what is left of the lush farmland and woodlands of Dane and Sauk counties. As I enjoyed the scenery and our conversation, it didn't cross my mind even once that I might win some money that afternoon. The closer we got to Ho Chunk, the more animated and excited Bev became. "We gonna have fun," she assured me. "We gonna win us some money today, girl!"

As we turned into the casino's sprawling parking lot, I was immediately struck by the building's design. The architecture suggests the southwestern pueblo style I had come to love during the annual pilgrimages the poet and I made to Taos and Santa Fe. The casino's exterior is painted in soft adobe colors and trimmed in turquoise and aqua blue geometric designs. I suddenly wished I was somewhere else, back in New Mexico getting ready to go on a long hike. But those days were over. The poet would no longer guide me along the trails in the mountains surrounding the Taos ski valley or in the Rio Grande Gorge as he had done for so many years. He wrote a poem to commemorate my first descent into the intoxicating and sage-sweet gorge. I was happy then. And in love. But now, with the architecture of Ho Chunk provoking such sensuous memories, I felt miserable as I followed Bev out of the sunny afternoon and into the crowded, noisy, and garishly lit casino. I wanted to be outside, enjoying the weather, going on a hike—anything but hanging out in this place.

"Well, okay, show me what to do," I said as Bev led me through rows and rows of slot machines.

"Let's walk around for a few minutes and look for some good machines," she instructed.

"What makes one machine better than another?" I asked. "Don't they all do the same thing? Take people's money?"

"Now, Sandy, you gotta think positive. We are going to win us some money today! You don't want to be sending out negative vibes to the machines."

Oh, boy, I thought. Now I'm supposed to believe these machines can feel my vibes.

Bev cheerfully showed me some of the more popular machines and explained how playing the slots was a form of relaxation for her. I couldn't understand how this could possibly be relaxing, what with all the noise, cigarette smoke (neither of us smokes), and the often irritating behavior of the other slot players. But Bev's beautiful face was calm; she was smiling. She was already having a good time and we'd just gotten there. Bev finally settled on some machines that allowed us to alternate between quarter and dollar bets. She told me to start by hitting the 25-cent button. I did that for a while and watched as the hundred-dollar bill I'd put into the machine got smaller with every touch of the button. A man at a machine across from me got up and left, and Bev told me to play his machine. It was a chili pepper machine. I withdrew the voucher with what was left of my hundred dollars on it and did as I was told. I hit the Bet Max button a couple of times, and three brightly lit red chili pepper symbols landed on the payline.

Suddenly, the machine started making a lot of chiming noises. People who had been playing other machines came rushing over to watch as the numbers on the payout monitor increased. When the payout stopped at $1,180, the machine's recorded voice congratulated me. I took my voucher to the cashier's counter and was paid in hundred-dollar bills. I hadn't been in Ho Chunk more than half an hour, had wagered less than $100, and had won $1,180. Talk about easy money! I was ready to go, but Bev was just getting started.

Bored, I walked around for a while. I bought a hotdog and a Heineken, which I drank right from the bottle, even as I realized how pissed I would've been if I had gone to a restaurant or bar and was not offered a chilled mug. What I would otherwise have considered unladylike behavior—slugging beer from a bottle as I walked around—seemed perfectly appropriate in this place.

Before I knew it, I was back at a slot machine. I reasoned that since I'd won what for me was a lot of money, I could risk the rest of the $200 I'd brought with me. I quickly lost the $180 and my interest in gambling, but Bev still was not ready to go. I tried to find a quiet place to read. I never go anywhere without a book and can usually read no matter what's going on around me. But not in a casino. I cannot tune out the incessant noise. It rankles my nerves. And the cigar and cigarette smoke! It's everywhere, stinking up my clothes and hair. Finally, about two hours after we entered, Bev was ready to leave. On the way home Bev talked about my beginner's luck and how her own luck was hampered by a woman at a neighboring machine who kept trying to talk to her. She said the woman broke her concentration.

"What's there to concentrate on?" I asked.

"Oh, on the way the symbols fall, the way your machine's acting," she explained.

"Oh," I said.

I was speechless. There isn't anything to concentrate on when you are sitting in front of a slot machine. But as I was soon to find out, serious slot players don't want to be bothered while they're trying to commune with their machines. They don't even want anyone sitting next to them. It's distracting to have people around when you're trying to make your machine give you money, lots of money.

That night I experienced what would become a habit whenever I gambled. I couldn't sleep. I kept asking myself, "Why did you sit there and lose that money?" I had reasoned that since the $1,180 I had won was not in my budget and was not what I consider a legitimate wage— something I earned through work—and since I had come out so far ahead, I could afford to risk losing $180, especially with the lion's share safe in my fanny pack. But that line of thought didn't make sense. Money is money. Money pays bills and I had quite a few to pay. After tossing and turning for most of the night, I decided that I would never go back. Gambling—winning quick money— is seductive. *Addictive* might be a better word. Nope, gambling was not for me.

The next morning I deposited my winnings in my checking account and tried to forget about Ho Chunk. But I kept seeing those chili peppers lighting up bright red and landing on the payline. The sound of the machines kept ringing in my ears. And I kept worrying about the $180 I had lost. Next time I'll be smart and leave as soon as

I win some money and not sit there like a fool and lose it back. *Next time?* There wasn't supposed to be a next time.

◆ ◆ ◆

Tuesday, May 17, 2005

I did a really crazy thing on Sunday. I went to Ho Chunk and lost almost $300. I'd brought only about $60 and lost that quickly. Then I took out a $200 cash advance on my credit card. I managed to build that up to $267 and lost it all. I need to get a grip on things. This is crazy.

◆ ◆ ◆

Thus began what I convinced myself was a binge: a gambling binge that would soon subside. Instead it grew worse over the summer, causing me a great deal of anxiety and stress. Even when I won, I worried about the bad habits I was developing, like taking out cash advances on my credit card.

Before I started gambling, I never even carried credit card balances in order to avoid paying interest. Now I was paying the exorbitant fees charged by the casino's money store and the 24 percent interest on my credit card for cash advances. And I was going to Ho Chunk more frequently, sometimes two and three times a week. It didn't make sense. I was wasting money and time doing something that was not fun in a place I disliked.

The day I lost $300, all I could think about was what I could've done with that money, like buy three theater tickets so my sisters, Brenda and Aloma, and I could see Denzel Washington in *Julius Caesar* during an upcoming trip to New York.

Several weeks earlier Brenda, who lives in Southfield, Michigan, suggested that we visit Aloma in New York and go see Denzel: a big evening out in the Big Apple. I told them I couldn't afford it. The round trip airfare was almost $400; a ticket for a decent seat at Broadway's Belasco Theatre was more than $100. Then I went to Ho Chunk and won $1,180. I called my sisters and told them about my win and that I was coming to New York. What I didn't tell them when I got there was that I had gone back to Ho Chunk two days before and lost $300.

We had a good time in New York. We went to the play and to dinner afterward. We talked about how great Denzel was as Brutus. I thought the actor who played Cassius was a bit too wimpy for a murderer. My sisters listened politely while I expounded about the play, acting, developing a character, and so forth. After a while they started rolling their eyes at each other, so I shut up and ate my food and let them talk some. We were happy to be together in the City. But when the check came, all I could think about was the money I had wasted on the slot machines.

My sisters paid the bill while I sat there wondering, for the umpteenth time, why I'd gone back to Ho Chunk and lost that money. It wasn't like I didn't have other, better, and less expensive things to do. Springtime in Madison always draws me outdoors: to jog, to walk, to plant flowers in my yard and hope they don't die. To spend Saturdays in Genesee Depot leading tours at Ten Chimneys, the country retreat of the legendary stage actors, Alfred Lunt and Lynn Fontanne.

I told my sisters about Ten Chimneys and all the famous theater people who went there to frolic with Lunt and Fontanne: Noel Coward, Katharine Hepburn, Laurence Olivier, Carol Channing, the acerbic theater critic Alexander Woollcott, the novelist Edna Ferber, the playwright Robert Sherwood, and the Lunts' very best friend, the actress Helen Hayes. After we finished our dinner, Aloma walked Brenda and me over to the Lunt-Fontanne Theatre and then to the Helen Hayes Theatre. I was happy.

♦ ♦ ♦

Since 1999, when I fell in love with acting, I've immersed myself in that world, taking every opportunity to develop whatever talent I might have and to establish myself as a specialist in U.S. theater history. It didn't bode well for my relationship with the poet. I was liberating myself intellectually, artistically, and spiritually, not only from the poet but from the weight I had borne for many years as a black woman professor at a predominately white university. It was stifling. I had achieved the goals I set for myself when I came to Madison from Detroit in 1983. I had educated myself against tremendous odds. I had earned a Ph.D., received tenure, published books and articles on African American literature, and had done all the other things professors are supposed to do. I had nothing more to prove to myself or anyone else in academia. In turning to theater I was responding to a passionate call from deep within me. The artistic side of my being was screaming to be allowed to emerge. Those Saturday visits to Genesee Depot invigorated me and kept me focused as my relationship with the poet burst wide open and finally revealed to me the mess I had been living with for a very long time.

Like most people in Wisconsin, I didn't even know Ten Chimneys existed until the estate was about to be sold and destroyed to make way for expensive condominiums. Tucked away on sixty wooded acres about thirty miles west of Milwaukee, Ten Chimneys was rescued in 1996 by a Madison businessman who helped to restore the estate and turn it into a national monument.

Ten Chimneys was my refuge. During the winter of 2004, I went to Genesee Depot every Saturday morning for fourteen weeks to learn how to be a docent. It was a rewarding experience. After years of studying and teaching African American theater history, I had finally established enough distance between me and the way my people were misrepresented in American theater and popular culture, especially during the first half of the twentieth century, to allow myself to branch out and soak up the rich history of Ten Chimneys.

I started leading tours in April of 2004. Every Saturday morning I left Madison for that enchanted world. I loved roaming around the estate, which once was a working farm, telling the stories I'd been trained to tell and adding a few of my own, which I'd gleaned from reading biographies of the Lunts and their famous friends.

Two weeks after I returned from New York, I went back to Ten Chimneys for the 2005 season, but my enthusiasm had waned. I was distracted. Genesee Depot is about a ten-minute drive from Potawatomi Casino in Milwaukee. After my tours I now found myself struggling to go back to Madison. I'd ask myself, "Why ruin a perfectly beautiful day by going somewhere and doing something I don't like? What's wrong with me?"

◆ ◆ ◆

Monday, June 6, 2005

There truly is seduction in gambling. I can see how people get caught up in it and lose their livelihoods. Saturday, after I finished my tours at Ten Chimneys, I went to Potawatomi Casino. In less than ten minutes I lost $50. I timed it. All I can say is that I had sense enough to leave right away. But I'm mad at myself for going there in the first place. I had a nice time at Ten Chimneys. Then I went to Potawatomi. That trip ruined my day. I should've headed straight back to Madison. I could've bought some flowers with the $50 and done something constructive, like plant them in the yard. Then, last night, I went to Ho Chunk with Bev and won $6,000! I started with $300. If I'd been alone, I would've taken my money and gone home. But Bev had come to gamble and wasn't ready to leave. So I took $5,500 in a check and $500 in cash and continued to feed the slot machines. I broke even, that is, I lost $500 and won it back. I didn't tell Bev about the jackpot. She's never around anyway. I don't know why she insists that she can't go to Ho Chunk alone. Nobody's going to rob her. As soon as we get there, she says good-bye and disappears. She'd stay all night if I didn't start complaining. I can't understand how she can spend hours looking at cherries and chili peppers and who knows what rolling round and round. And the noise. It never stops.

◆ ◆ ◆

Winning that jackpot was a strange experience. Back in April, when I won on the chili pepper machine, I was at what's called a progressive machine, one with a big jackpot and a progressive payout—the jackpot continues to grow as people feed the machines, often running up into hundreds of thousands of dollars and occasionally spitting out smaller wins. The chili pepper machine's escalating tones signaled that I was a winner. The people who left their machines to see what mine was doing watched excitedly as the numbers on the LCD monitor marched toward $1,180. I didn't like it one bit when they looked over my shoulder at my winnings. I was glad when the attendant brought me my money and those people went back to their own business. But the sound of the progressive machine! It stayed in my mind for months.

I won the $6,000 jackpot on a five-times-pay machine, what industry insiders call a flat-top slot. It has a fixed rather than a progressive payout. I had been at the machine next to it and had gotten bored with losing my money there. After watching several people sit at the one to my right, spin a few times, and then leave, I decided to give it a try. I might have hit the Bet Max button two or three times. (Always bet the maximum if you're going to bet at all. Or so sayeth the gambling gurus.)

Suddenly, three symbols lined up on the payline. The machine started making a rapid pulsing sound, and a white light on top of the machine began blinking. People quickly gathered around. The monitor lit up and read "Call Attendant." I pushed a button on the monitor, but nothing happened. I pushed the Bet Max button again. Nothing happened. "What's wrong with this machine?" I was talking to myself, but the man next to me leaned over and said, "You just won the jackpot!"

"What do I do now?" I asked.

"Just wait. An attendant will be here soon to give you your money." I tried to push the "Call Attendant" button again, but nothing happened. The man next to me assured me that someone would soon be along.

"Just sit and wait. Don't leave your seat," he advised.

So I sat and waited while people came by to see what I had won.

"She just won $6,000," one woman said.

A man said, "Well, I'm glad somebody's winning something here. I've been here for three hours and haven't won a dime." He put his hand on my shoulder and said, "Good for you!"

Someone else said, "Good job!"

Good job for what? I wondered as I sat there nervously hoping the attendant would hurry and the man would take his hand off my shoulder and go blow his cigar smoke somewhere else. I had nothing to do with the outcome of this game. It was a random event, totally out of my control. I didn't use any special skills or magic wands to make those symbols fall on the payline. That jackpot happened because deep inside the machine is buried a tiny computer chip called a random number generator. The random number generator is working all the time, even when the machine is not being played. Push the (Bet Max) button or pull the bandit's arm, and the computer stops on three numbers that correspond to the symbols and blank spaces we see on the machine's screen. It's all random; there's nothing magical about slot machines. There's lots of illusion, though. The symbols and spaces we see on the screen, the images that are so mesmerizing, so addictive, give us the illusion that the jackpot is just another spin away. If you're at the right machine at the right time, it'll happen.

"THAT'S A BIG FIVE TIMES WIN!" the voice in my machine hollered to everybody around me. As I sat there waiting for the attendant, I felt none of the euphoria and excitement that gamblers report experiencing after a win. Instead I felt numb and anxious. Somewhere deep inside me a warning signal was going off, alerting me that winning so much money so quickly is dangerous.

Two attendants finally arrived, and everyone settled back down in front of the machines and kept right on playing, with even greater intensity, or so it seemed to me. One attendant opened the machine and wrote down some numbers on a form while the other took my driver's license and asked me to fill out a W-2G form. Jackpots of $1,200 and larger are considered income and must be reported to the IRS. Great, I thought. Now I'm creating a paper trail. Now the government's in the act, taking its share of my money.

The woman attendant asked me how I would like my money—cash or check. I couldn't imagine someone counting $6,000 in hundred-dollar bills into my outstretched hand—they tell you to please hold out your hand for a hand pay—so I asked for a check for $5,500 and the rest in cash.

It took about twenty minutes from the time those three brightly lit symbols fell on the payline for the attendants to complete the paperwork for the check. I was impatient and nervous. I knew that if Bev came along while all this was going on, we'd never get out of there. And I wanted to go home. I tucked my winnings into my fanny pack and went looking for her.

She was at her favorite spot, the "I Love Lucy" machine. She said she was losing and wanted to try to win some of her money back, just another forty-five minutes, she promised. I left and went to the wild cherry machines. An hour later, after losing and winning back the $500, I finally told Bev that we really needed to leave. We had been there about three hours and I just couldn't stand it any longer. As we drove back to Madison I vowed never to return. When I deposited $5,700 in my checking account the next day, I had all I needed to get through the summer, $12,000.

Bev complained all the way home about how Ho Chunk is just a rip-off place and how those machines weren't doing nothing but taking people's money. I didn't say a word. Of course, it's a rip-off. Gambling is for fools; everybody knows that. Slot machines take in enormous amounts of money and occasionally give some back. After all, casinos would go out of business if they didn't have winners. Economists who study the gambling industry estimate that about 70 percent of the more than $48 billion casinos rake in annually comes from slot machines. That's why casinos dedicate so much floor space to them. Most slot players lose. Increasing numbers of them—many of them women— suffer enormous losses so a few others can win. I had gotten lucky, I suppose.

What troubled me more than Bev's ranting and raving about how much money Ho Chunk had stolen from her were my thoughts. I wanted to go back. It didn't matter that I was unlikely to win such a large jackpot again. Worse, while I'd been giving back the money I'd just won, I reasoned that I could afford to risk $500 because it was money I wouldn't have had if I hadn't come to Ho Chunk in the first place. That's the kind of reasoning people who design and operate casinos count on. I had to remind myself that no matter how I acquired it, it was my money I was playing with, real money. Not play money. And money pays bills.

I returned home that evening exhausted and worried. Why did I sit there and risk that money? I decided that I needed to stop going with Bev since she would sit there for hours if I didn't keep bugging her about leaving. But Bev wasn't the problem. Although I wasn't willing to admit it, I had begun to look forward to her calling and saying, "Let's take a ride."

CHAPTER 2

The Mighty River

Two days after I won the $6,000 jackpot at Ho Chunk, Bev called. She wanted to try the casinos in Dubuque, Iowa. Someone had told her that in May a woman won $750,000 there. I told her that I'd be by to pick her up. I figured that if I drove, she would *have* to leave when I was ready to go.

Dubuque is a quaint and picturesque river town about ninety miles southwest of Madison. It's not exactly a place I would go out of my way to visit, but I had passed through it often enough when the poet and I traveled to Taos to anticipate a rush of excitement as I drove across the Dubuque-Wisconsin Bridge with its panoramic view of the Mississippi River and the stately Victorian architecture that makes up Dubuque's cityscape.

"Look, honey!" he would say to me as we drove along the bridge. "There it is, the Mighty Mississippi!"

This time all I felt was agitation. I hardly noticed the view. My magical Mississippi moments were gone along with the poet. I had come to Dubuque to gamble. I'd withdrawn $500 from my checking account for the trip to Iowa. I immediately lost it at the first casino in Dubuque. I had a bad feeling about being there anyway, at the Dubuque Greyhound Park and Casino, where they race grey-hounds. I had bad vibes about the dogs, about running those spindly legs to death so people can bet on the dogs.

I felt sick after I lost that money and was ready to go home, but Bev wanted to try a riverboat, so we went to the Diamond Jo Riverboat Casino. This was my first time seeing a riverboat up close. I didn't say anything to Bev, but I didn't want to enter it. I knew too well the history of riverboats and slavery. Riverboats like the Diamond Jo once transported enslaved African Americans down the Mississippi to the southern slave markets and plantations. An inner voice kept warning me that I had no business being there, but I followed Bev into the Diamond Jo nonetheless and descended into the boat's dark lower deck. It was early afternoon and the place was packed tight with slot machines and elderly white people, women and men who looked like they had just stepped out of a commercial for Blaine's Farm and Fleet Country Store. The air was rank, the noise from the machines mind numbing.

Bev lent me $300. I lost most of it, then won it back and repaid her. After about an hour we decided that the riverboat wasn't going to give up anything and went back to Ho Chunk. I was broke again so Bev lent me $300. The same thing happened. I nearly lost it all, won it back, and repaid her. I had $40 left. It was about 2 a.m. I passed a ten-times-pay gold bar machine on my way to the restroom and inserted a twenty-dollar bill. I hit the Bet Max button a couple of times and two gold bars dropped onto the payline along with another winning symbol—I don't remember which one. The light on top of the machine started blinking rapidly. I'd won $2,000.

This time I sat quietly and waited for an attendant. No crowd gathered. I was paid in cash. I forgot to tell the attendant that I wanted a check, and she said that she couldn't go back and redo the transaction, so I held out my hand and she counted out $2,000 in hundred-dollar bills. I was ready to go. I found Bev at the "I Love Lucy" machine. She was almost broke. This time I told her that I'd won, mainly because she'd lent me the money to keep playing. I gave her $200 and sat at the machine next to hers and lost another $200 before I managed to convince her to leave. It was now after 3 a.m. We had spent the whole day running from Wisconsin to Iowa and back to Wisconsin to gamble. I was exhausted from all the driving and embarrassed about my behavior. I thought, "Next time, I'll go by myself. Bev keeps telling me this is relaxing and that she enjoys playing the slots. Well, I don't. I've got to get away from this. It isn't healthy."

No matter how much I tried to convince myself that gambling was not the way I wanted to spend my time and money, by mid-June I was going to casinos two or three times a week. I went to Potawatomi Casino in Milwaukee just three days after the Iowa excursion. I'd gone to Schamburg, Illinois, for a commercial print audition and had every intention of going straight back to Madison. Instead, I stopped at a bank, withdrew $300, and went to Potawatomi. I won quickly on a "Wheel of Fortune" machine and left with $1,000. I would've had $200 more if I hadn't stayed and tried another machine. Anyway, I felt a sense of urgency as I drove home. I just wanted to get the money in the bank. I now had more than $14,000 in my checking account, $10,000 of it from gambling. There was no reason for me to keep going back to the casino and risking what had come so easily, enduring enormous stress in the process. I knew this streak of luck couldn't last forever, but every win was an incentive to go back and try it again. I was trapping myself in what would later become a cycle of wins and losses. I was also becoming afraid.

◆ ◆ ◆

I started doing commercial print modeling in the late 1980s after someone recommended me to a local talent agency. As one of the few black women on the Madison campus at the time, I stood out. I wore hats. I still do. I was also very thin so people just assumed that I modeled. Nobody made that assumption in Detroit where I was born and raised and where skinny, hat-wearing black women are a dime a dozen. But this was lily-white Madison, Wisconsin, where black folks are few and far between. I signed on with the talent agency and occasionally got called to do a print advertisement for Cuna Credit Union or some other business that had finally realized it needed to show a black person in its ads every now and then.

I didn't take modeling or acting seriously then. I had to get my Ph.D., get a job and tenure, and write some books. Plus, Madison isn't a strong enough commercials market for it to be worth the money and effort to get good headshots and photo composites. You have to go to Chicago to break into the national commercials market, and Chicago is two and a half hours away. That meant spending five hours driving along I-90 for a five-minute audition.

Everything changed in 1999 when I was asked to be in a short skit celebrating the university's sesquicentennial. The students in the Master of Fine Arts program in acting were putting it on, and they needed an African American woman to play a returning adult student. The director called and asked if I would do it. She assured me that all I had to do was sit at a table and say a few lines. Well, that was easy enough. After all, I'm a university professor. I'm good at sitting at tables and talking. I agreed, but it was an ordeal. Sitting and saying a few lines turned out to be about motivations, objectives, and truthfulness—about being believable and breathing life into this character I was supposed to be portraying, et cetera, et cetera.

Most of the time I had no clue to what the director was saying to me, so I did what I usually do when I don't understand something. I went to the library and got a book on acting fundamentals. After about a week of rehearsals, things began to make sense. I knew which way to go when the director told me to move upstage or downstage, and I had begun to create an inner life for this character. By the night of the performance my anxieties and frustrations had ceased; I was enjoying myself.

The play was part of the entertainment for a benefit dinner for the university. When I peeked through the curtains and saw who was in the audience—university administrators and their wives and friends all dressed up and looking like penguins and peacocks, I thought to myself, "Why, they don't scare me. I'm going to go out there and do my thing." And I did.

Something happened. It was like magic. The lines, the engagement with the other actors—all graduating MFA students—were all there. For about twenty minutes I experienced what it was like to inhabit another being.

After it was over the director said to me, "Sandy, you've got something there. It's rare to see someone with no experience break out like that. So, when are we going to see you on stage again?" I swore that I would never do it again. It was too stressful—running from class or a committee meeting to rehearsals. Being embarrassed because everyone in the rehearsal room seemed to know what was going on except me. Being stared at as I struggled with my lines. A week later I was reading the audition notices in the paper.

Thus began my acting career. I performed in local community theater, learning by doing and flying by the seat of my pants until I got to a point where I knew that, if I was going to be any good at this, I needed professional training. I signed up for classes at the Audition Studio in Chicago, and for the next five years I drove from Madison to Chicago and back once a week for acting training. Not once did I notice a big billboard hovering over I-90 for the Grand Victoria Riverboat Casino in Elgin, Illinois. Not until the summer of 2005. Then I saw billboards for casinos everywhere.

◆ ◆ ◆

The first time I took the billboard's advice and tried my luck at Illinois' most popular casino, I was surprised that the Grand Victoria Riverboat was a showboat. The stately white-and-red gingerbread-trimmed riverboat is docked on the Fox River opposite an expensive condo development and looks like a replica of the boat in *Showboat,* Jerome Kern and Oscar Hammerstein's musical about the Cotton Blossom Floating Palace Theater and its troupe of dancers, actors, lovers and gamblers. Only this showboat, like just about every other riverboat casino, doesn't go anywhere. It sits tightly moored at the waterfront in downtown Elgin, its entryway a cavernous land-based structure attached by a walkway to an enormous parking structure.

I lost $90 in less than fifteen minutes during my first trip to the Grand Victoria and decided that this showboat was not for me; if I was going to continue gambling, I needed to go where the odds seemed to always be in my favor—to Ho Chunk.

◆ ◆ ◆

Monday, June 13, 2005, 11:35 p.m.

I'm tired. I went back to Ho Chunk today. I took $250 out of my savings account. I got there around 5:30 and left after 10 p.m. During that time I won and lost about $900. I deliberately fed the machines. I felt like the only way to break this hold that gambling had on me for the past couple of weeks is to go all the way—win and keep putting money into the slot machines until I lose it all back. That's what compulsive gamblers do.

◆ ◆ ◆

As my gambling increased, so did my irrational thinking about what I was doing. I honestly believed that I was somehow helping to break the spell the slots had on me by losing the money I'd just won. Instead of leaving after I'd accumulated six hundred-dollar bills, bringing my fanny pack stash up to $900, I sat at a ten-times-pay machine and started feeding it, $100 at a time. I felt like a crazy person. The man next to me complained that he had lost $1,800 on the ten-times-pay machines. He was angry; I was disgusted with him and me. I felt like yelling at him, "Will you shut the fuck up?"

Here I was, losing more money than many of the employees at Ho Chunk earn in a week. I looked around at the slot attendants, bartenders, and blackjack dealers who, by that time of night, looked like they were bored out of their minds and wondered, "What's it like for them to stand around watching people throw away so much money?" They obviously have to be here, in this unhealthy place— dark, smoky, and noisy. I don't. I have choices. For one thing, I could've taught a four-week class during summer session and earned the money I needed. Instead, and for reasons I didn't understand, I chose to indulge in risky behavior as a route to financial stability. That choice was impulsive rather than rational. It was informed by the ever-present possibility of the great reward—the jackpot. It was reinforced by the smaller wins—hundred-dollar bills at the press of the Bet Max button—the space of the casino itself, and the encouragement the ever-beckoning machines dole out to slot players. They call out to us from the casino's every nook and cranny: *"You're a winner! Come on! Let's play!"*

That night I experienced the first of the slot-machine-induced nightmares that for months disturbed my sleep and left me exhausted the next day. I was in a cavernous and empty casino and couldn't find my way out. Everyone had left. There were no floor attendants or security guards to point the way out. I felt so claustrophobic that I could hardly breathe as the slot machines morphed into ugly and menacing creatures. Everywhere I ran I confronted a walking, talking slot machine, its jackpot symbols lighting up on the payline, the numbers running up, up, up. The sounds of the progressive payouts kept getting louder and louder. Suddenly, the ten-times-pay machines exploded, releasing millions of hundred-dollar bills. They knocked me off my feet. I lay there on the floor, covered by a mountain of money. My heart pounded rapidly. I couldn't breath.

My dream frightened me so badly that when I woke up I couldn't get back to sleep. I just lay there, exhausted. The sounds of slot machines reverberated in my mind. Whenever I closed my eyes, I saw brightly lit jackpot symbols so vividly that I felt like I was still sitting in front of the machines. What I didn't know then was that slot machines have a mesmerizing effect on some people, overriding their ability to think, to be rational about what they're doing. It certainly was irrational for me to think I could break what was becoming a bad habit by losing money. I told myself that I was teaching myself a lesson: that compulsive gamblers will lose in the long run. And they will lose big. But I didn't think of myself as a compulsive gambler back then. I just knew that something was happening to me that didn't make sense.

Later the next day I stopped by my office to pick up a few books and ran into my colleague, Michael Thornton. Michael is a sociologist. He and I share a common background and sense of purpose as academics. We both come from a poor or working-class background and are committed to working with inner-city undergraduates who might have difficulty adjusting to an environment in which, more often than not, they'll be the only person of color in the room. I asked Michael if he'd ever played slot machines. He said that he did once, during a trip to Las Vegas. He went to a casino, lost a few dollars, and that was it. He doesn't like wasting money. He also said that he likes playing video games and knows he could easily become addicted to something like slot machines.

That was the first time I heard the word *addicted* used to describe gambling behavior. But then, before the summer of 2005, I never thought about gambling at all. It wasn't on my mental radar. Now it was all consuming. It was all I thought about. I was worried—*afraid* might be a better word.

I told Michael about how I'd gone to Ho Chunk and won and, for a brief moment, fancied myself queen of the slot machines. I also told him about my previous night's experience at Ho Chunk and about my dream. As irrational as it seems to lose money like that, I told him that by doing so I'd purged myself of whatever it was that had taken hold of me. I was never going back.

"I wouldn't be so confident about that," he responded. "Gambling is totally irrational, and the whole enterprise is set up to seduce people, especially people with addictive personalities. That's the way casinos are designed."

I left Michael's office thinking, "The man is an eternal pessimist. And did he just say that I have an addictive personality? How would he know? He could've been more reassuring."

Truth be told, I've struggled with alcohol addiction for most of my life. I also once was a heavy smoker. I started smoking at age fourteen and for the next twenty years or so I smoked at least a pack of unfiltered Pall Mall cigarettes a day. But I didn't think of what I was doing as addictive behavior back then. Most people didn't. Smoking was acceptable. Acceptable for grownups, that is. The last thing I wanted was for my parents to catch me with a cigarette hanging out of my mouth. I was just trying to be cool, part of the in-crowd, a little Detroit girl trying to look tough by smoking cigarettes and occasionally drinking VO whiskey. Straight, no chaser.

It was difficult, but by my mid-thirties I had defeated my addiction to cigarettes. I finally quit smoking, and I drank alcohol only occasionally, usually white wine. I can go for months without touching a drop of alcohol, then go on a binge. But during my professional career I've shown up tipsy or drunk at enough events for people who know me to be concerned, especially if I was driving. My tolerance for alcohol is high, dangerously so. So I stopped driving whenever I wanted to go drinking. I took a taxi or got someone to drive me home.

Unlike gambling, alcoholism is an addiction that's difficult to hide. Gamblers can hide their addiction from their family and friends, and they usually do until it's too late. They can disappear into the casino, lose themselves deep within the labyrinth. The alcoholic can't. More often than not, when she imbibes, her addiction is placed on display, in all its ugliness. Addictive behavior is also repetitive. The addict keeps doing the same things, making the same promises to herself: "I'm going to stop."

Occasionally Michael Thornton invites me to speak to students in his "Introduction to Sociology" class about my experiences as a nontraditional adult student from Detroit who never even attended high school— I became pregnant at fourteen and quit school after completing the ninth grade—and the obstacles I had to overcome in order attend college and eventually, after years of work and study, earn a Ph.D. and a faculty position at a major research university.

I don't go into great detail about my early life. I focus instead on how I managed to get into college after earning a G.E.D diploma, how I financed my education, and the strategies I used to overcome my academic deficiencies. I encourage the students to stay focused, study hard, manage their money wisely, and never, ever forget from whence they came.

When I visited Michael's class during the fall semester of 2005, I felt as if I were talking to myself. I was the one who needed to hear what I had to say. I was playing such a dangerous and destructive game with myself that I needed to remember from whence *I* came.

CHAPTER 3

Detroit

Before I arrived in Madison, Wisconsin, in 1983, I had never lived anywhere outside Detroit, where I was born. In the early decades of the twentieth century, Detroit was a city of greater opportunities for black people than the places from which they migrated. My parents moved to Detroit in 1940. My father was from West Virginia, my mother from Kentucky. They were part of the second wave of the Great Migration, the mass movement of black people from the rural south to northern industrial centers such as Pittsburgh, Gary, Indiana, and Detroit that began in the 1890s and continued until after World War II when those cities' economies began to decline.

Relatively speaking, Detroit was a good place for a young black man to be in 1940. Despite the rampant racism that kept the majority of black people confined to overcrowded and substandard housing in inner-city neighborhoods and in domestic service or on dangerous and filthy factory jobs, Detroit in the 1940s practically guaranteed steady employment for anyone who wanted it. Of the Big Three auto makers—Ford, Chrysler, and General Motors—the Ford Motor Company was most aggressive in recruiting and employing black men (and during the war years, women). Most of the men, fresh from the South, had little or no education. They were laborers, stuck in the lowest paid and most dangerous jobs, with no chance for advancement.

My father worked in Ford Motor Company for only a short while. He hated being in the factory. When he heard that a downtown parking lot was looking for attendants, Daddy left Ford and never went back. He worked for more than twenty years as a parking lot attendant at Patton Garages in downtown Detroit, picking up cars from the major hotels and parking them for the hotels' guests and permanent residents.

How my father managed to support a wife and four children on a job that paid mainly in tips is beyond me. My mother didn't work outside the home. My father wouldn't allow it. The only employment available to black women was domestic work. He would often say, "As long as I have a breath in my body, no wife of mine is gonna be scrubbing some white woman's floors. I'm taking care of this family." We lived in a five-room flat on the North End, on Cardoni Street, a stable black neighborhood where the only white people we ever saw were the fresh produce and fish vendors, the milkman, and bill collectors.

Compared with other families in the neighborhood, ours was fairly stable, despite my father's womanizing. Sometimes when Daddy left Momma the car, a big green Hudson Hornet, she would get us all dressed up—my brother, Jimmy, my sisters, Aloma and Brenda, and me—and take us to the garage to meet Daddy after work. We loved going there. Daddy looked so handsome in his uniform, a dark blue shirt and pants and a dark blue captain's cap. The highlight of our visit was when Daddy took us for a ride in the garage. He would drive real fast, speeding around the curves all the way to the top floor and back down as we laughed and cheered and begged him to do it again.

Daddy usually worked a late afternoon shift. Sometimes he didn't come home until morning. One night Momma went to the garage and caught him with another woman. The woman had short hair. Momma came back home, went into the bathroom, and cut off her long, wavy black hair.

My mother died in 1992 after a two-year battle with multiple myeloma, a cancer of the bone marrow. I wasn't there when she passed, but Brenda told me that during those last few days, as our mother drifted in and out of consciousness, her thoughts were on her husband. Although they had been separated for years, she never gave up hope that they would be together again one day. He visited her regularly while she was in the hospital. If he wasn't there when she awoke from her morphine-induced stupor, she would ask, "Where's James?" It only added to Brenda's grief; she couldn't understand it. After all the years of loneliness and neglect my mother endured, how could she love this man so deeply? Brenda told me that sometimes she wanted to say to our mother, "You're dying and you're asking for him? What has he done for you? What has he brought to the table?" Instead, Brenda went to her just a few days before she died and asked her to leave this earth. By then Momma was in terrible pain, her bones so brittle they could hardly sustain the weight of what was left of her body. "I told her that she had been a good mother and that there was nothing left for her to do here. I asked our mother to let go," Brenda said. Almost to the very end, Momma kept asking the same question: "Where's James?" My mother loved my father to the end of her life. I loved him, too.

Daddy held me all the time. One evening while I was visiting him during the 2006 Christmas holidays, he said to my sister Carla and me, "Sandra Ann was an easy child compared to Brenda. Sandra Ann would be awake at 2 a.m. when I came in from work. She'd just be lying in her crib watching me. I'd pick her up and give her a bottle, and she'd go back to sleep. Brenda was the opposite. She cried all the time. All you had to do was look at her and she'd start crying. And on top of that, she swallowed a safety pin—a big diaper pin—and we had to take her to the hospital."

Fortunately for my sister the safety pin was closed and passed right through her little body. But the story of the safety pin and the comparisons my father made of Brenda and me over the years made one thing clear: I was his favorite child. That favoritism did great harm to my sister, that and her firm belief that she was an unwanted child, that Momma and Daddy never loved her. She told me recently, "You were dainty and cute, an easy child to love and care for. I was ugly. Momma didn't want to be bothered with me, so she shoved me off on Aloma."

For years I was the standard against which Brenda was measured. I was studious. I loved to read and almost always got all A's in school. I was involved in after-school activities such as swimming. I took dance lessons at the local recreation center, got involved with theater, and never had any problems being alone as long as I had something to read. Daddy had great expectations for me. When I became pregnant just two months before my fifteenth birthday, my father unleashed all his anger, pain, and disappointment on Brenda.

We were living on St. Clair Street, on the East Side. Daddy had bought a house in a predominately white working-class neighborhood. I had my first encounters with racism there. On Cardoni racism was never an issue. Everyone there was black, and we rarely ventured past our neighborhood. In our North End neighborhood we were free to just be little kids playing in the street.

St. Clair Street was a different matter. White children weren't allowed to play with us because we were colored. St. Clair Street soon became a totally black neighborhood. As quickly as black families moved in, white families moved out. This was during the mid-1950s. The same thing was happening in northern cities across the country: black people moving in, whites fleeing.

The house on St. Clair represented a major accomplishment for my father. He was now a property owner. But it was not a happy home. There now were two more children: Frank and Carla. Daddy complained constantly about not having enough money. As we grew older, he began nagging us about getting a job to help out.

Like my older brother and sister, I got caught up in my father's complaints about money. I really wanted to help, but there were no jobs for a fourteen-year-old girl, not even babysitting. People in our neighborhood rarely went out. When they did, usually to a church-sponsored event, they took their children with them. When a neighbor mentioned that he needed a dishwasher at his restaurant, Daddy agreed to let me work there a couple of hours each night after school and on Saturday afternoons. I earned about ten dollars a week. I felt very grown up because I was helping out.

As it turned out, I was feeling a bit too grown. I had just started the ninth grade. Since I was the brain of the family, everyone expected me to go to Cass Technical High School, where the most gifted and talented kids in the city were enrolled. They also expected me to be the one to go to college, to Wayne State University or the University of Michigan in Ann Arbor. Instead, I ended up back on the North End.

◆ ◆ ◆

The restaurant was in an old hotel on the corner of Holbrook and Greeley, about a mile from where I was raised on Cardoni. Compared with where I now lived, this part of the North End was not pretty. The houses were old and needed painting and repair. Few had lawns or gardens. The dirt yards were littered with garbage and junk. A huge General Motors factory dominated the cityscape.

Every day after school I took the bus there and spent the evening standing on a little wooden platform, my skinny arms elbow deep in a big sink full of soapy water and dirty dishes. We served the men from the factory's late shift good old home-cooked food: beans and ham hocks, beef stew, fried chicken, mashed potatoes and gravy, greens and neck bones, cornbread with butter, pig tails and pig feet and sauerkraut. I was a novelty among the men—a cute and proper little girl with two long braids hanging down her back—"jailbait," as they jokingly called me.

In addition to the men who came to eat dinner before returning to work, there were the numbers runners who stopped in every day to take bets after making their rounds in the hotel and the boosters who darted in and out trying to sell watches and rings and whatever else they had stolen that day. These activities were new to me. I had stepped out of my safe, working-class community and into one where people had to run a hustle to make it through the week. I knew nothing about gambling or numbers running or boosting until I started working at that restaurant in the hotel at the corner of Holbrook and Greeley.

The restaurant's cook played the numbers daily. I learned from her the language of the numbers business: single action bets, combinations, boxing a number, getting a hit, winning a pot. During slow periods the cook would come from behind the steam table, sit on a counter stool, pore over a raggedy "Lucky Red Devil Dream Book," and write down her numbers on a little slip of paper. She once explained to me that dreams have lucky numbers. All you have to do is look up your dream in the dream book and find its number. If you dream about money, then you play the money row, five sixty-seven. Dream about a dead baby and you play a combination of the baby row, one-twenty, and the death row, four-one-three. She never gambled with much money, usually a quarter, occasionally a dollar. I don't know if she ever won anything, but she spent a lot of time trying.

Gambling was going on in back of the hotel too. A group of young men who hung out in the alley often engaged in a vigorous game of craps while drinking wine and smoking reefer. One day one of them came into the restaurant to buy a Coke. He winked at me. I smiled back. Then he started coming in every evening to buy a Coke. He would sit and drink it and watch me as I stood on the little platform and washed the dishes.

One evening I got the bright idea of shortening the plaid skirt I was wearing by pulling the waistband way up on my body so he could get a good look as I bent way over, farther into the deep sink than was necessary to wash the dishes. I had also worn two pairs of wool knee socks so my legs would look bigger. It worked. The next day he told me I had pretty legs. He asked me how old I was. I lied and said I was fifteen going on sixteen. He was twenty-one, and although I didn't know it until after I had become pregnant, he was also married and had a two-year-old child. All I knew was that this was a grownup man, not some silly boy, and he was interested in me. He thought I was cute.

This was 1961. In those days people didn't talk about sex, not our mothers, that is. And there was no such thing as sex education, unless you count the movie that was shown in the physical education class that had something to do with an egg and a sperm meeting somewhere in some dark and damp place and a baby appearing nine months later. We might as well have seen a movie about how a stork brings babies from heaven and gently drops them in cabbage patches, for all we learned from these weak efforts to teach young girls about sex.

By the ninth grade the girls in my homeroom talked about sex all the time, trying to figure out how babies really get born and sharing all kinds of misinformation, the most damaging that you can't get pregnant the first time you do it, whatever *it* was. Some girls started bringing in pictures of boys and men they liked and passing them around. It was like a big game, everybody showing off these older boys and men and talking about how they were doing *it* with them.

In retrospect, I think most of those girls were only boasting, but this new interest in *it*, along with my desire to fit in, my raging hormones, and my ignorance about sex and men, turned out to be devastating for me and my family, especially for my sister Brenda.

Somehow I got it in my head that sex with an older man would be okay since he would know what to do. After all, he had experience. Plus, he had been in the army and was a paratrooper, jumping out of airplanes and stuff. At least that's what he told me. I was just a stupid little girl, and he took advantage of my ignorance. I knew nothing about contraceptives; I had never even heard the word. Knowledge of contraceptives wouldn't have helped me, anyway, since it was illegal in most states to sell them to young unmarried girls. It was even illegal during the 1960s to distribute information about birth control, sexually transmitted diseases (STDs) or anything else that had to do with sex and sexual behavior. It was just assumed that good girls like me wouldn't let themselves get into trouble. Never mind that our interest in sex was maturing along with our bodies. All I knew was that what this man was doing to me felt good and I didn't want him to stop.

I have often wondered over the years if by engaging in sex at such an early age I was rebelling against my father's infidelity. His womanizing was no secret. He often hurt and disappointed us by not coming home when he said he would to take us on a family outing, causing my mother to go into a rage about whatever woman he was running around with. Sometimes my mother would try to block him from leaving the house. I hated to see her crying and pulling on my father's coat sleeve as he headed out the door, begging him not to go out on weekends, when he regularly left her at home to carry on his affairs with other women. As my siblings and I grew older, we each found a way to escape from all the unhappiness.

I escaped at age fourteen through sex with a twenty-one-year-old man. I started skipping school to be with him. We had sex as often as we could: in his mother's house when nobody was home; in the backseat of his father's old broken-down car that was parked in their backyard; in one of the rooms that was rented out for that purpose in the after-hours joints he took me to; on a blanket in the park at Belle Isle—anywhere we could do it without getting caught. And since I didn't know any better, I trusted him when he promised me that he wouldn't get me pregnant; he would be sure to pull out in time. During the 1960s young men were making that promise to thousands of young girls across the nation. They lied; we got pregnant. Conservative estimates place the annual number of out-of-wedlock births between 1960 and 1965 at 250,000, of which about 41 percent involved girls younger than nineteen.

♦ ♦ ♦

In May of 1961, I missed my period. At first I wasn't worried. I believed what my boyfriend said about how he would be careful and not knock me up. I graduated with my class from the ninth grade, but by mid-June I knew that I wouldn't be going to high school. I had missed another period. I couldn't deny it any longer. I was pregnant. Still, I was hopeful that things would turn out okay. I had read lots of stories in *True Romance* magazine about girls who got in trouble, married the boys who got them pregnant, and lived happily ever after, so I believed the fairy tale would happen to me, too.

It never occurred to me that the girls in the magazines were white and that the reality was that thousands of white girls in this country were not living happily ever after, that many were either having illegal abortions, giving up their babies for adoption, or finding themselves hopelessly trapped in shotgun marriages with no way out.

When I broke the news to my boyfriend, he told me not to worry; he knew what to do. Medical abortions were still illegal and would remain so for another twelve years, until the U.S. Supreme Court ruling in *Roe v. Wade* in 1973. And I had read enough stories to know that illegal or back-alley abortions were both dangerous and costly, and we didn't have any money. So he was going to help me induce one, as if that were safer than going to an abortionist. He bought me a bottle of something called Humphrey's 11 and told me to drink it all at once and that would take care of the problem. All it did was give me a bad case of diarrhea.

When that didn't work, he took me to his sister's house and gave me a pint of VO whiskey. He said that if I drank it all really fast, I wouldn't be pregnant anymore. The whiskey would kill the baby growing in me and it would come out when I went to the bathroom. He stood there, urging me on, as I drank the whiskey as fast as I could. I got very drunk and started running around his sister's apartment, laughing and throwing up all over the place, while she tried to get me into the bathroom. She finally got me into the bathtub and started throwing cold water on me to sober me up. When she found out what we were trying to do, she called us both damn fools and ordered him to take me home. I was terribly sick the next day. And still pregnant. So the only thing left was to tell my parents I was pregnant and that we were going to get married and live with his family.

I'll never forget that night. My father was sitting in the living room in his favorite chair reading the newspaper and drinking a bottle of Pabst Blue Ribbon beer. I introduced him to my boyfriend and said, "Daddy, we have something to tell you." He looked at me, smiled, sipped his beer, and asked, "What's that?"

"I'm pregnant, Daddy." Daddy was silent for what seemed like an eternity. Then tears welled up in his eyes. His voice was quiet at first. He asked my boyfriend, "So what're you going to do about it?" My boyfriend lied and said: "Well, I love her and I'm going to marry her." "No, you're not," my father yelled. "That girl is only fourteen years old and the law won't allow it. Your ass is going to jail if I don't shoot you first!"

Daddy ordered him out of the house. Then all hell broke loose. Momma was in the basement ironing while this was going on. Daddy called her upstairs and said, "This girl done gone and got herself knocked up." Momma started crying. She slapped my face and started yelling at me: "How did this happen?" I decided to get smart with her: "How do you think it happened?" Another slap across the face. Daddy went on and on about how this n—— is going to jail. They kept asking the same questions over and over again: "How did you go and get yourself knocked up? What you doing out there, sleeping around with somebody like that? You better say something, girl, before I beat the life out of you." The more they yelled and screamed, the more I clammed up. I finally was allowed to go to my room, the one I shared with my sisters Aloma and Brenda.

The next few days saw a great deal of yelling, crying, more slaps across the face as my parents interrogated me: "How many times did you have sex with him? Where did it happen? Did you do it with anybody else? How could you do such a thing? We trusted you, and now you done gone and shamed us all, this whole family."

One afternoon after I shut myself up in the bedroom, my mother, in one of her rare moments of affection, came into the room and lay on the bed next to me and put her arms around me. "Tell Momma what happened. How many times did you have sex with him?" I turned my head away from her and toward the wall. "I don't know, Momma." She asked, "Sandy, why did you do this?" I told her I didn't know. I couldn't tell her that I did it because it felt good. In those days girls and women weren't supposed to enjoy sex. If they were married, it was their duty to have sex with their husbands. If not, they weren't even supposed to think about it. If sex was on your mind, it meant that you were loose, promiscuous, a slut, whore, unfit to be around good girls and boys. Momma cried and kissed me on the cheek and left me lying there on the bed feeling so ashamed.

A few days later Daddy took me to juvenile court. We met with a little gray-haired white woman; I believe her name was Mrs. Sorensen. She was one of many social workers I saw over the next few years. All were white. Mrs. Sorensen had a motherly manner, but the others were horrible. They treated me like dirt. I sat in Mrs. Sorensen's office and tried to tune out everything she and my father were saying until I heard her say something about statutory rape. *Rape?* That's when I spoke up. "He didn't rape me. We love each other, and we're going to get married."

Then reality struck. Mrs. Sorensen explained that I was under the age of consent, only fourteen and therefore a child. This man was twenty-one, and, according to Michigan law, it was illegal for us to have sex, even if I agreed, since a child is incapable of making such a decision. My boyfriend had committed a crime and could be prosecuted under Michigan's statutory rape laws. The laws were intended to protect young girls like me from manipulative men like him. He could go to jail for two to fifteen years, depending on the charges.

As I listened to Mrs. Sorensen explaining procedures to my father—there would be an investigation, my boyfriend would be arrested and prosecuted, I would have to testify in court—I decided right then and there that I would not cooperate with my parents and this lady who wanted to put my boyfriend in jail for something I let him do. I was to blame for everything since I lied and told him I was fifteen going on sixteen.

I decided that the best thing for me to do was disappear. If they couldn't find me, they had no victim and therefore no crime. The problem was that my parents wouldn't let me leave the house. One or the other was constantly watching my every move. I hadn't begun to show, but they made me stay inside anyway. My mother told me that if anybody came to the house, I was to stay upstairs in the bedroom. They didn't want anybody to see me. I was now unfit to be around kids my age, so I stayed in the bedroom with my sisters as my only company. One night I got Brenda to help me escape.

Our house had a small porch off the upstairs bathroom. I pretended to be asleep until everyone else had gone to bed. Then Brenda helped me climb down the drainpipe leading from the porch to the backyard. She dangled her legs over the edge of the porch to give me something firm to hold on to as I slid down the pipe. I ran through the alley and headed straight to my boyfriend's sister's house, walking clear across town in the middle of the night. She let me in but told me I couldn't stay; I would have to go back home.

I don't think I'd been there more than a couple of hours when the police came to get me. I begged her not to let them in. There was nothing she could do; she opened the door and stepped aside. Two uniformed policemen and a plainclothes policewoman entered. One of them asked, "Are you Sandra Ann Qualls?" I shook my head yes. The policewoman walked over to me, took my arm, and said, "You must come with us." They put me in the backseat of the cruiser and took me to the juvenile detention center—to jail. I stayed there a week.

The other incarcerated girls were sympathetic toward me. Most were there for more serious offenses: prostitution, shoplifting, assault. A few had mental and emotional problems that sometimes flared out of control. Fights were frequent. When I told the girls why I was there, that my father had me arrested because I was pregnant and had run away, and that when I got out my boyfriend and I were going to get married and go live with his family, they agreed that I was being treated really badly. After all, when did getting pregnant become a crime?

Shortly after I was released to my parents' custody, I got another reality check. Mrs. Sorensen and her investigators learned not only that my boyfriend was married but also that he had a criminal record: he had been arrested on several occasions for minor offenses. I was devastated. He had been lying to me all this time about the girl I sometimes saw with him as he passed by the restaurant. I thought it was strange that he never stopped in, didn't even wave when he was with her. I once asked him about her, and he told me it was his sister. I had no reason to believe otherwise because she resembled his sisters, at least from afar. He later admitted that she was his wife and they had a two-year-old daughter, but they were separated. After they got a divorce, he was going to marry me and we were going to live with his family until he got a job and got on his feet and could take care of us and get us an apartment with some new furniture, and he was going to buy some nice things for me and the baby because he *loved* me.

A further complication was my mother's announcement that she too was pregnant. My brother John is three weeks younger than my oldest child. There now was no way I could stay in the house. My father said, "I can't have both of you here pregnant. You can't stay here. You got to go." But where?

When my paternal grandmother, Grandma Armstead, visited that summer, she begged my father to let her take me back to West

Virginia. She thought it would be good for me to be in the country. I would be with my aunts and cousins, and after the baby was born someone would be there to take care of it while I went back to school. I had just turned fifteen and liked the idea of going back to school in a place where nobody knew me. My father wouldn't agree to let me go. He said that all I would do was cause her trouble. No, he wasn't going to put this burden on his mother. I was going to have this baby and put it up for adoption.

Grandma Armstead tried to reason with him: "Son, this isn't something colored people do. We don't give our babies away. We can always find a way to feed one more child. Let me take her home with me. She can stay with me or Barbara Jean, and we'll help raise this child." I also pleaded with him. "Daddy, let me go." He wouldn't budge.

After my grandmother left, he admitted that the real reason he didn't want me to go to West Virginia was because his sister, Barbara Jean, wasn't married and had a houseful of little bastards running around everywhere and didn't know who the daddies were for half of them. She would be a bad influence on me since I was just like her and couldn't seem to keep my dress down and my drawers up. I was going to stay right here and have that baby and give it up for adoption.

◆ ◆ ◆

I don't know where my father came up with this idea about adoption. I think it might have been Mrs. Sorensen or our family doctor who suggested that my father send me to the Florence Crittenton Home for Unwed Mothers and that I should relinquish my child at birth. Anyway, one day he took me to the home. It was in a black, middle-class neighborhood on the northwest side, at 11850 Woodrow Wilson, right next door to Crittenton General Hospital. The home didn't look much different from the juvenile detention center. It was a drab, three-story rectangular brown brick building with windows you couldn't see into. The only difference between it and the detention center was that it didn't have a high brick wall around the recreation area. It was fenced in, though, another jail as far as I was concerned. (Today the building houses the Cass Community Social Services Organization and provides shelter for the homeless.)

A social worker took me upstairs to a large room where I was introduced to several pregnant girls. She didn't give them my name; she just said that I was a prospective new resident she was showing around. All the girls where white, just like in the *True Romance* magazine stories I liked to read. In fact, between 1960 and 1965, of the 250,000 teenage girls who were getting pregnant each year, about twenty-five thousand white girls from working- and middle-class families spent their last trimester in homes for unwed mothers and gave their babies up for adoption, not because they didn't want them but because so much pressure was placed on them from everyone involved to do the right thing and give the child to a deserving childless couple who could give it a better life.

That social worker started in on me right away after she asked me to step into her office. She assured me that at the home I could continue my education, learn some hobbies, and be with other girls just like me. Except they weren't just like me. The girls I met that day were white, and as stupid as I was at that time, I knew it was highly unlikely that a deserving childless couple would want to adopt my little black baby. I had never heard of any black child being adopted or of any black people who had adopted a child. Nope! They weren't about to get my baby.

I sat there and looked straight in front of me as the social worker talked about how I could go back to being a regular teenager after I gave up my baby. I could put this all behind me as if it never happened, go to high school, get a job after graduation, and maybe even get married and have another child when I was older and better able to take care of it. I tuned her out, just as I had Mrs. Sorensen when she kept going on and on about putting my boyfriend in jail.

About a week after the visit, my father informed me that I wouldn't be going to the home after all. He couldn't afford to send me. Instead, I would go there regularly as an outpatient for prenatal care and counseling. I would have my baby at Crittenton General Hospital and give it up for adoption. That was the plan. But there was one problem. Nobody could *make* me give up the baby. When the social worker told me I had to sign a paper relinquishing the baby, I asked, "What if I don't sign it?" She said, "Nobody can force you to sign the paper and give up your baby, but how would you take care of it? You have no education, no skills, no job. You'll just end up on welfare and become a burden to the taxpayers. It's really in the best interests of the child to give it up to a deserving childless couple who can give it a good life, blah, blah, blah—." *Tune-out time.*

I began to hate that woman. Every time I went for a checkup, I had to stop by and listen to her go on and on about how I would be doing something very selfish if I didn't give this baby away. I was supposed to go to her office for counseling right after my checkup. The counseling session basically amounted to her saying the same things, why I should relinquish this baby. It would be best for us both. It would be hard at first, but I would eventually forget all about it and go on with my life. After my second checkup I left without keeping our appointment. By the time I got home, she had called my mother and said she was changing the appointment time. I would now have to see her *before* I had my physical examinations. I knew it was important to get regular checkups, so I abided by the new rule. I would go to her office and sit looking straight ahead of me or down at my fingers, trying hard to not let what she said penetrate my consciousness. I tuned her out as best I could.

It was different with Mrs. Sorensen. She was such a kind-looking lady. She acted like she really cared about me. I had regular appointments with her. She would ask me how things were going at home, what I was doing with my time—by that time I had retreated deeply into the large collection of paperback books my mother kept on a shelf in the basement—and was I still seeing my boyfriend. Since he never kept a steady job and stayed at his mother's house just long enough to get some sleep before heading back out into the streets, they couldn't find him. I lied and told her no, but the truth was that I would sneak out whenever I could, usually after one of these appointments, and meet him in one of the after-hours joints where he hung out. His friends— petty hustlers, prostitutes, moonshine merchants, numbers runners, and gamblers—liked me. I guess that since I was so young, so proper, and so out of place in those back-alley joints, they found me a bit of a novelty. My boyfriend did, too; I was his little girl. And he *loved* me.

◆ ◆ ◆

On January 13, 1962, I woke up with a rolling pain in my stomach. It would subside for a while, then start up again. I was in labor. My father got up, bathed, shaved, and got dressed. He smelled so good; my daddy always smelled good. It was his birthday. He was taking his fifteen-year-old daughter to the hospital to give birth on his birthday to his first grandchild. Daddy dropped me off at the entrance to the Crittenton General Hospital and left. I went through labor and the birth of my first child alone. I knew from my prenatal visits what to expect in terms of the physical experience of giving birth: the pains would come more frequently, my water would break, there would be a bloody show, and then a baby would be born.

What I didn't expect was the hostility of the doctor who delivered my baby and the indifference of the people who assisted him. Aside from the nurse who came in periodically to check on me and give me ice chips to suck on, no one made any effort to comfort me. I suffered alone. I suffered quietly, every pain a punishment for my crime of being an unwed mother.

As I was being prepped, I begged the nurses not to give me anything that might put me to sleep. I was afraid the social worker who had been assigned to my case would take advantage of the situation and get me to sign the papers she was always sticking under my nose. Finally the ice chip lady came in with the doctor. He examined me and said, "She's ready. Let's get her into the delivery room." As I was being wheeled out, a woman in another room who had been making a terrible racket started yelling, "This is unfair! I was here first! Why are you taking her? I was here first!"

Only one word can describe the way I was treated during that delivery—cruelly. The doctor and interns who examined me during my prenatal care weren't particularly kind, the doctor less so than the interns who were allowed to poke around inside me, but this was something else. The doctor who delivered my daughter acted like he was angry, like this was a great imposition on his time. He kept telling me to push, but I couldn't. I had been given an epidural when the pain became unbearable, so I couldn't feel the lower part of my body, and no one had ever explained how I could be actively involved with bringing this child into the world. All they were interested in was my giving her up for adoption.

"Aren't you going to help at all?" the doctor asked. "Push," he ordered. "Push what?" I wanted to know. It would have helped if I had known what to do, but my prenatal care didn't include birthing exercises. He made some angry remarks about all these young girls having babies. I don't remember exactly what he said, but it made me feel very bad. Even as I was giving birth to a healthy baby girl, I was being reminded that I was no good, an unwed and unfit mother.

The doctor used forceps to bring her out and dropped the little wriggling, whimpering thing on my stomach. "Here's your baby," he said. He cut the umbilical cord and left. The nurses cleaned her up and took her away, leaving me lying there alone, my legs still in the stirrups. I don't know how long I lay there like that. By the time a nurse came to get me, I was shivering. The others hadn't even bothered to cover me with a blanket before they left.

Someone finally wheeled me out of the delivery room to the ward reserved for unwed mothers. Except for me and another black woman, all the other women in the room were from the maternity home. They were white. And they all relinquished their babies. I was adamant when the social worker arrived, not even hours after I had given birth, to pressure me into signing her damn papers. I refused.

The other black woman was the only one who was allowed to have her baby in the ward. She was the oldest among us. She told our nurse that she didn't know why she had been sent to this ward since she had been married, was divorced, and was having her second child. The nurse simply said, "Then you're an unwed mother," and went about her business of getting the rest of us ready to have our breasts bound.

It was very painful. The nurse wound a long, narrow piece of white cotton cloth around our chests, wrapped it tightly in the back, and secured it with large safety pins. By binding our breasts she was suppressing our milk, denying us the experience of being lactating mothers.

Years later I read that breast binding is recommended for mothers who lose their babies during childbirth or while they are still lactating. In addition to suppressing their milk, breast binding is somehow supposed to aid them in their grief, according to the experts who study such things.

But our babies didn't die. They were right down the hall from us, in the nursery where we were allowed to see them only through the window during restricted hours, after the families of the "legitimate" babies had come and gone. We weren't even allowed to touch them. Just stand there at the window and watch them. That's all we were allowed to do.

Two days after I gave birth, I began having urinary problems and had to be catheterized so many times that I developed an infection. I became so feverish and weak that I couldn't walk down the hall to the nursery window to see my baby. Another girl told me that she overheard a nurse complaining that I must not care about the baby since I hadn't asked to see her for two days. I felt helpless, lonely and ashamed. Not only was I in pain from the binding on my now engorged and leaking breasts; every effort to urinate brought more pain.

One night I became so feverish that the nurses had to put cold cloths and ice on my body. The next morning they moved me into a single room. Fortunately, I slept a great deal or the pain and loneliness would have been too much for me to bear. My mother was my only visitor during my sickness. I was so happy to see her. She said that she and my father had come to get the baby and that my sister Aloma would help take care of her until I came home.

I spent ten days in the hospital. Aloma told me years later that she didn't know that I remained in the hospital because I was very ill. She thought I was locked up in the maternity home. She remembers my mother sitting with my baby in the backseat of the car and looking down every few minutes at her granddaughter. Aloma was in the front seat; Daddy drove, looking straight ahead. Nobody said anything. Aloma remembers that nobody ever said anything about me while I was away. I was a taboo subject. They just didn't talk about me.

My daughter was eleven days old before I held her in my arms for the first time. I fed her with a bottle since I had no breast milk. My mother taught me how to take care of her. I worked alongside her, helping to take care of my daughter and my brother John, who was born three weeks after my first child.

CHAPTER 4

Locked Down

My parents did the best they could with this difficult and embarrassing situation. But it was too much for everyone, both financially and emotionally. I never found out how the expenses for my maternity were covered. I'm certain my family received no public assistance. My father took great pride that we were never on welfare or any other form of public aid. We were all healthy. My mother made sure we had regular medical and dental checkups. We always seemed to have what we needed. My father somehow managed to make ends meet.

But two babies in the house were more than he could handle. To make matters worse, my baby cried all the time. Aloma said that she was fine as long as someone was holding her. But the minute you put her down, she would cry. I often wonder if this had to do with her being separated from me so early in her life. There was now so much tension in the house that my father would often rage about how I had ruined this family and how, since I was the one who went out and got herself into trouble, I needed to help support this child.

Since I wasn't able to enroll in high school at mid-semester, I applied for a work permit and got a job downtown washing sundae and soda glasses behind the lunch counter at Woolworth's five-and-dime on Woodward Avenue. Whenever I could, I took my baby and slipped away to see her father. I wanted him to hurry up and get his divorce so we could get married because things were unbearable at home. My father really wanted me and my bastard child out and would say so just about every day. I got pregnant again. I was still under age, fifteen years old, and pregnant with my second child.

This time my parents took more drastic actions. They met with Mrs. Sorensen at the juvenile court and started procedures to turn me over to Michigan's juvenile justice system as an incorrigible child, a "status offender," according to Michigan law. As soon as they told me what they were going to do—make me a ward of the court and put both me and my baby in foster care—I started making plans to run away. I thought that if I could stay away until I turned sixteen, my parents couldn't have me locked away again. They also would have to drop all charges against my boyfriend, whom they were still trying to prosecute. I was wrong. The age of majority in Michigan was eighteen, not sixteen, but I didn't know that then.

One day, when everyone was out of the house for one reason or the other, I wrapped up my daughter, put a few baby clothes in a bag, and left. I had no money, just enough bus fare to get me to the North End, to the home of a friend of my boyfriend, a woman named Lillian, whom I had talked into letting me stay with her. I told her that my parents had put me out and told me to never come back. Lillian saw to it that I had food and shelter and never let any of the men who hung out at her place approach me in any way. I earned my keep by taking care of her children and trying to keep the place clean.

Lillian was very pretty. She was a big woman and wore brightly colored muu-muus and gold hoop earrings. She looked exotic to me, like whatever image I had at the time of women on Caribbean islands. Lillian spent her days playing bid whist and poker with the men who came to her house, drinking Pepsi, eating potato chips, and smoking cigarettes. She was about thirty-three and had six children, all of whom had different fathers. The children were always dirty. She rarely bathed them because she didn't have hot water. She hadn't paid her utility bills in months, so they were disconnected. We heated our water and cooked our food—usually a pot of pinto beans or collard greens—on a big potbellied wood-burning stove that stood in the dining room of Lillian's five-room flat. We used kerosene lamps to light the rooms.

This was a level of poverty I didn't know existed in Detroit before I started living in it. It didn't have to be that way. Lillian acted like she didn't care. Her children did well while I was there. I played with them, something Lillian rarely did. I read to them whenever I could find a book or magazine in the house and helped them with their homework. I gave them regular baths. I washed and combed their hair and washed their clothes on a washboard. I tried to keep the house clean, but it was hopeless. Lillian never bothered to teach the children to clean up after themselves. I stayed there only a few weeks. She finally got tired of my complaining about the filth and told me that maybe I should find some place else to live.

My boyfriend arranged for me to stay with a woman who sold moonshine out of Gerber baby food jars and was in the numbers racket. Since there were men coming in and out all day and night to place their bets and buy corn liquor, she made me and the baby stay in an upstairs room most of the time. She didn't want nobody messin' with "that little girl," as she often referred to me. Occasionally my boyfriend stopped by with some milk or clothes for me and the baby that his mother had bought from the Goodwill. He never stayed long, though. He often disappeared for days and reappeared long enough to leave some food and clothing, rarely any money, because he didn't work anywhere.

One night I woke up with a horrible toothache. During the next few days it grew worse. My caretaker tried her best to ease the pain. She ground up an aspirin and instructed me to put it in the big and throbbing cavity. When that didn't work, she soaked cotton balls in corn liquor and had me hold them on the tooth. She gave me codeine. Nothing helped. Every night I lay in my bed, moaning and writhing in pain. Finally, when I could no longer bear it, I went to a nearby phone booth and called Mrs. Sorensen at juvenile court and asked her to help me get to a dentist. She wanted to know where I was. By this time I had been away from home about two months.

"Sandra, where are you? Are you with your child's father? Do you know where he is?"

"I'm not with him, but I can't tell you where I'm at, Mrs. Sorensen. I just want you to help me get my tooth pulled. It hurts so bad I can't stand it anymore. I just want you to help me get it taken out."

"All right, dear. Come to my office and bring the baby, and I'll get a dentist to take care of you."

"Thank you, Mrs. Sorensen. I'll be there in about an hour."

"Okay, dear. But Sandra, be sure to bring the baby with you. I'd love to see her. I'll have someone take care of her while you're getting your tooth pulled."

I thanked her again and went back to the house and asked my caretaker for bus fare to Mrs. Sorensen's office. She told me not to take the baby, that she would keep her until I came back. She didn't argue when I said that Mrs. Sorensen wanted to see her. She gave me the money and went back to watching the soaps. I never saw her again.

The bus ride to Mrs. Sorensen's office was pure hell. Every bump in the road sent a pain reverberating through my head. I was so relieved when I arrived at her office that at first I didn't notice a woman standing outside her door. Mrs. Sorensen remained seated behind her desk as she asked me a few questions.

"Aside from the tooth, are there any other health problems?"

"No, ma'am."

"Where have you been all this time?"

"I can't tell you, Mrs. Sorensen."

"Were you with your boyfriend?"

"No, ma'am."

"Do you know where he is?"

"No, ma'am."

"Did he get you pregnant again?"

"No, ma'am."

"Sandra, are you lying to me?"

"No, ma'am."

"Are you telling me that you've been promiscuous with other men?"

"Yes, ma'am."

"Sandra, who got you pregnant this time?"

"I don't know."

"You don't know? Sandra, I think you're lying."

After a few minutes the office door opened and two women entered. They were plainclothes policewomen. I recognized one of them from the first time I was detained.

"Sandra, give the child to Mrs.————."

I started crying. "Mrs. Sorensen, why did you lie to me? I just need to get my tooth pulled! Please don't take my baby from me. Please!"

I held on to my child as the policewoman tried to get her out of my arms.

"Please, Mrs. Sorensen, don't let her take my baby!"

Mrs. Sorensen didn't move.

"Sandra, give the baby to Mrs.————. We're not taking her from you. We just want the doctor to have a look at her. We need to make sure she's in good health. You've been gone a long time, you know."

"Please, Mrs. Sorensen! Please!"

I never relinquished my child. That woman took my baby. She yanked her out of my arms and carried her out. After she left, Mrs. Sorensen informed me that I would be going back to the detention home. Since my parents couldn't control my behavior and I refused to cooperate in prosecuting the man who got me pregnant, and since I was still under age, a minor in the eyes of the law and an incorrigible child, I was being detained for my own good. The policewoman who remained in the office with us took my arm and led me out of Mrs. Sorensen's office, through the hallway to the adjacent detention home. I was ordered to strip, only she put it rather nicely.

"Now, Sandra, you've been here before, haven't you? Undress and take your shower. We'll get you some clean clothes, and get you on over to your floor."

In the 1960s girls occupied two or three floors of the juvenile detention center. I was back in jail.

It was a few days before I got to see the dentist. He came to the center only once a week. He was more cruel than the doctor who delivered my baby. A bald-headed, short and fat white man, he made no effort to be gentle as he jabbed a needle into my lower gum and released the novocain to numb it. When I complained, he said, "Look, girlie. Do you want this tooth out or not?" I nodded yes. I was barely numb when he started yanking on the tooth. I tried to tell him it wasn't numb yet, but he ordered me to shut up or he would just leave the tooth where it was. The pain was excruciating, but he got the tooth out. He cleaned the wound and lectured me about how we girls should be grateful to get this free service. For years afterward I had a terrible fear of dentists. In my mind they all were like this mean, bald-headed white man.

◆ ◆ ◆

I spent almost two months in the juvenile detention center—one month, two weeks, and five days, to be exact. I was there about a week before I met with a caseworker and found out that my baby was back home with my parents. I asked her when they were going to let me out. She claimed that she didn't know. Every week when we met, I asked her the same question: "When am I getting out?" Her response was always the same: "I don't know." Not once did she talk to me about teen sexuality, birth control, or parenting. Her theme was the same as that of all the other social workers I had to deal with: give the babies up for adoption so they can have a decent life.

Aside from meeting weekly with the caseworker and spending a few hours in class each day, I had nothing to do while I was in the juvenile detention center. The days were long and boring. We got up around 6:30 a.m., showered, and had breakfast around seven. Our food was served on metal trays, and we ate with spoons, the only utensil we were allowed to have since the girls were always fighting and trying to stab each other with whatever they could get their hands on. Classes were from 9 a.m. until noon. Then we had lunch and sat around until dinner. If the weather was nice, we were allowed outside in the recreation area. It was surrounded by a twelve- or fifteen-foot brick wall with barbed wire on top. There was no way to escape. We were locked in our little cinderblock cells at 9 p.m. At 10 the lights went out.

I experienced none of the ambience during this second visit that I did when I was first detained. I don't know what I did to alienate the other girls. By the second week I knew something was wrong. About twenty girls lived on the floor. Most afternoons they would be gathered on one side of the big common space, watching television, playing Scrabble or cards or gossiping. Whenever I tried to join them, they snubbed me.

After a while I stopped trying to make friends; I couldn't bear the rejection. I retreated into whatever books and magazines I could find. There wasn't much to choose from—*National Geographic*, a few novels. Our guard, or floor mother, as the guards liked to be called, sometimes gave me the crossword puzzles from her newspapers and, occasionally, a book to read. Since we weren't allowed to stay in our rooms unless we were sick, I spent each day sitting on one side of the room, all alone, while the other girls laughed and joked with each other and swapped stories about their crimes. Sometimes a small group of them sat quietly across the room and looked at me. Always the same girls quietly staring at me. They were threatening me but for what, I didn't know.

One day our floor mother called me into her office, a glassed-in room with a security door, and said, "Go get your bedroll and your personal belongings. We're moving you upstairs. We think you'll do better with the older girls." A guard came and escorted me to my new home. It was calmer there.

One day one of the girls asked me, "Do you know why they moved you up here?" I didn't. She informed me that some of the girls were planning to gang up on me in the shower and beat me up. That's why I was transferred. I tried to be tough. I pretended I wasn't scared or bothered by what she told me, but it made me feel really bad. I didn't know what I had done for the girls to want to beat me up.

The girl told me that she heard that they were going to teach me a lesson. They thought I had gotten too friendly with the floor mother and that I acted like I was better than the rest of them. I was a bit too uppity for them. I admit that I loved to talk to the floor mother. We weren't allowed in her office, but I would often stand in the doorway when she had her door open and talk to her about the books I read, about how much I really loved school, and about my baby. This girl warned me to stay away from the floor mothers from then on. And I did.

I made a few friends while I was there. One was named Sandra. She had been arrested for prostitution. She was seventeen and very smart, not at all like what I had been taught to believe about prostitutes. Sandra had grown up in foster care and had been in and out of detention homes most of her life. I told her about what was happening to me and she reinforced what I already knew—that I should do whatever I could to keep my baby out of foster care.

One day my father came to visit. I refused to see him. Sandra saw him sitting in the waiting room when she went to meet with her caseworker. When she came back, she said, "Sandra, your father is sitting out there crying. You shouldn't have done that." I told her that I refused to see him because he was the one who had me locked me up. "Yeah, but he's still your father. You shouldn't have done that." I felt so bad. My daddy didn't come back until I was released.

♦ ♦ ♦

My caseworker arranged for me to be released to my parents' custody on the condition that I not leave the house without their permission and under no circumstances have contact with my baby's father. She also set a date for me to appear in family court. Since I was an incorrigible child, I was to be made a ward of the court and sent away to a juvenile detention center outside the city and would remain there until I turned eighteen. That's what I was told. The babies were to be placed in foster care. I vividly remember my mother telling me, just a few days before I was to appear in court, that I had better get a good look when the new baby was born because I was never going to see it or my daughter again. She shook her finger in my face, her own face pink with rage, and called me immoral and said I was unfit to be a mother.

I believed everything she said. My court date was set for a Monday morning. I ran away that Sunday night and stayed away for more than a year. This time my boyfriend's mother helped orchestrate my disappearance. As much as she tried to cooperate with my parents to keep me away from her son, she couldn't accept the idea of losing two grandchildren. She arranged for someone to pick me and my daughter up that Sunday night and take us to Romulus, Michigan, where we would stay with an elderly couple she knew.

Romulus is only about thirty miles from Detroit, but in 1962 it might as well have been in another country. It was rural. Many of the homes had few of the conveniences I took for granted, such as indoor plumbing and electricity and gas. The old people who agreed to take me in lived in a two-room cabin. Although the place was neat and clean, it was far from quaint. It was old and leaky and cold at night. I slept on a cot in the room where the old people did all their living. A wood-burning cook stove kept the place warm. One of my jobs was to bring in wood from outside and keep the fire going. The old lady also wanted me to cook, but I didn't know how. I could hardly cook on a gas or electric stove, so I had no clue about how to cook on one that burned wood.

I hadn't been there more than a few days before the old lady turned hateful on me. She criticized me for everything I did wrong. Every morning I heard the same rant: "I've never seen such a stupid girl in all my life. Get out there and get some wood. I told you not to let that fire die down. Get out there to that pump and fill up those buckets and hurry back with the water. Hurry up!" Occasionally the old man tried to intervene. "Leave the child alone. Can't you see she's trying?" That just made matters worse. One night she accused me of trying to steal her man. She yelled and screamed obscenities at me until I couldn't take it any longer. I lay on the cot with my hands over my ears trying to block out the horrible name-calling. I cried myself to sleep. The next day I told her I was leaving. She said, "Good riddance."

I put a few baby things in a bag, wrapped up my daughter, and walked about a mile along a dirt road until I came to a highway. I had no idea where I was or in what direction I needed to go in order to get back to Detroit. I just knew I had to get away from the old woman. I don't know how long I stood there with my baby before a car came along. A woman was driving. She stopped and asked me why I was out there all alone with the baby. I'm sure I looked a mess, a frail teenager in a filthy and loose gray dress with black buttons down the front, my face dirty and tear-streaked, my hair uncombed. When I explained to her what had happened, she took me to her house, called my boyfriend's mother, and told her she was bringing me back to Detroit. She knew the old lady and said that everyone around there thought she was crazy (in fact, she suffered from dementia). A few days later my boyfriend found another place for me to stay. One of Lillian's friends, Doug, agreed to let me stay with him and his wife, Mattie, in exchange for housekeeping chores and babysitting duties.

Doug and Mattie were good to me. They made sure I wasn't over-worked, that I got enough to eat, and that my baby was well taken care of. They also tried to talk to me about my boyfriend. Doug knew him well. They often went to Lillian's to play cards, but Doug had a regular job and always took care of his family. Mattie warned me that my boyfriend wasn't going to amount to much. He didn't work, and wherever he went he started a fight. He had a terrible temper. It seemed that whenever he came around, something—maybe the sight of me and my skinny pregnant body—would trigger his anger, and I'd end up with a fist in my face. Afterward he would promise to never do it again. But it happened again. Many times.

Mattie tried to get me to see that there was no future with him and that if I kept running back to him, I would just end up pregnant again, maybe dead, since he was always beating on me. She encouraged me to think about my babies and my future. "Look at Lillian," she often said. "You don't want to end up like her, do you? A woman in her thirties with six kids and living on welfare and not knowing who her babies' daddies are. You don't want to end up like that, do you?" No, I didn't. For years I told myself, "I've got to do something. I don't want to end up like Lillian."

◆ ◆ ◆

On December 5, 1962, I got up early and prepared to wash a bathtub full of dirty clothes. Mattie and Doug didn't have a washing machine, so I did the wash on a washboard in the bathtub. Suddenly I felt a familiar rolling pain in the lower part of my stomach. It subsided and I continued with the wash. By the time I had finished, the pains were coming more frequently. I was in labor. I waited until the pains were no longer bearable and told Mattie. Doug took me to the hospital and dropped me off. Three hours later my son was born.

For the second time I went through labor alone. As with my first birth, I asked for an epidural. I wanted to remain awake and alert. I was eager to see my baby as soon as he was delivered. I watched the whole thing on a big mirror hanging above the delivery table. My mother's words echoed in my ears: "You'd better get a good look at that baby because you're never going to see it again." I also wanted to make sure he was okay, that he had all ten fingers and toes, because I'd had no prenatal care with this pregnancy. I was a runaway. People were looking for me. If they found me, they were going to take my babies from me. So I stayed away from hospitals and clinics. I didn't have money to pay for medical care anyway. When the time came, I simply walked into a hospital—I don't remember which one—announced that I was in labor, and had my baby. The physician and nurses didn't treat me badly, but they weren't comforting, either. They just went about doing their job. When it was all over, they sent me to the welfare ward. I was sixteen, the lone teenager in a ward with women who were referred to as "welfare cases."

The next day a white woman came in with some papers for me to sign. She asked me my name and a lot of other questions that I refused to answer, like what was the child's father's name. I was afraid she had been sent from family court and was there to take my baby. I guess she thought I was ignorant when I wouldn't talk to her. When I finally told her that I didn't know who the father was, she got angry. "You're lying there, telling me you don't know who's the father of your child?" I turned away from her and closed my eyes. She grabbed her briefcase and papers and left.

Although I didn't know it then, she probably was there to register my son's birth. When I wrote the Michigan Department of Health's Vital Records Department in 1968 for a copy of my son's birth certificate, I was informed that there was no record of his ever being born. I had to file a petition with the court for a delayed birth registration. It was recorded and filed with the state on October 3, 1968. For six years my son didn't exist as far as the State of Michigan was concerned. That might explain why I was able to slip by the people whom I believed were trying to find me so they could take my babies, put them up for adoption, and lock me up in a detention home. Most of the major hospitals in Detroit had been alerted to my approximate due date. I got lucky. I pissed that lady off so badly that she didn't complete the job she was sent to do, and I walked out of that hospital with my little baby boy.

We were at Doug and Mattie's for only a couple of weeks. They had three children, the youngest of whom was only a few months older than my daughter. The new baby was too much of a financial strain on the family, especially since my children's father wasn't contributing anything, although his mother stopped by from time to time to bring us milk and clothes she had bought from the Goodwill.

Doug arranged for me to live with a friend of theirs who ran an after-hours joint in her basement. The lady needed someone to help with her children while she ran her business—an illegal drinking and gambling establishment. She lived in a two-story yellow brick house on Russell Street, right across from a big scrap iron yard. The area was industrial; small factories and metal shops made up its landscape. The house was a haven for me and my babies, tucked away in this industrial area.

Doug and Mattie had a good talk with me before they took me to my new home. They had found a safe place for me. I was safe from the people who wanted to take my babies from me; I was safe from the man who beat me. They made me promise not to tell him where I lived. I didn't. But I lived in fear while I was at the yellow brick house on Russell Street until I met a man named Richard Adell.

He wasn't a regular customer at the lady's after-hours joint. He came one night with a couple of other men to drink some corn liquor, shoot craps, and eat some of the soul food dinners we sold. I usually wasn't around much after the food was sold out. My main job was to stay upstairs with the children, away from the action. But that night I happened to be in the basement watching the craps game. Richard Adell asked the lady who the little girl was. She called me over and introduced us and then sent me upstairs.

For the next two weekends Richard came to the house. The lady ran her operations only on weekends, Thursday through Saturday nights. The rest of the week she worked as a domestic, but like so many other poor working black women, her salary wasn't enough to make ends meet. She didn't run the craps games, and I don't know if she took a cut of the pot for the poker games. She made her money on food—fried chicken and fish dinners, chitlins and greens and corn bread—and corn liquor.

Each time Richard Adell came to the house, he asked about me. Finally the lady let me come downstairs while he was there. He said that I was cute, that he liked me, and that he wanted to marry me and be a father to my children. I knew something was wrong with this man. He was thirty years old, almost six feet tall and as skinny as a rail, and had a mouthful of bad teeth. But he wanted to *marry* me. I was almost seventeen, had been away from my family for more than a year, and wanted to go home.

Richard took me and my babies to meet his mother and his aunt, who was the minister of a small storefront church. They liked me and were happy that their Junior had finally found a wife. Aunt Titi, as we called her, demanded that Richard get me and my babies out of that house of sin I was living in right away. We moved in with his mother and eight brothers and sisters. The five-room flat was on Cameron Street, just around the corner from Cardoni, where I was born. I became, for a short while, part of this large, extended, and totally dysfunctional family.

There was much praying and gospel singing in this house. Everyone had a beautiful voice. Richard sang bass in his family's gospel group. We spent most Wednesday evenings and all day Sunday in church. Yet for all her worship and praying, guidance and charity, Aunt Titi couldn't prevent the fights that regularly broke out between brothers and sisters, husbands and wives and lovers. Sometimes somebody would start fighting right outside in front of the little storefront church just minutes after a rousing and Holy Ghost–filled Sunday afternoon service.

The first thing I did after we moved in with Richard's mother was call my father. I told him that he had a grandson, that somebody wanted to marry me, and that I wanted to see him. He said, "Come on home, baby."

I'll never forget the evening I returned to the house on St. Clair Street. I was nervous. Richard carried my daughter and I had my son. My father wept when we walked through the door. My mother came into the living room and reached for her grandson. He grinned and drooled all over her as she hugged him.

I introduced Richard to my father, and we made arrangements for me to get married. Before we left, my father said he had to call the police so they would stop the missing person bulletin. This time I wasn't afraid. After all, I was going to get *married*. I would have a husband; I would no longer be an illegitimate mother. People would finally begin to respect me. Never mind that I didn't even like this man and that he was ugly and had horrible rotten teeth and was rather crazy. He was my ticket home.

Two policemen came. They asked to see the children. They asked if I was okay. One of them asked, "Where've you been? We've been looking for you for a long time." They told me that they had, in fact, given the major hospitals my description and the approximate date I was expected to deliver my baby. I reminded them that it's easy to disappear in a big city. They wished me luck and left. I was home at last.

CHAPTER 5

Welfare Mother

Richard Adell and I were married in Aunt Titi's little storefront church in the spring of 1963. My father and sister Brenda attended the wedding. My mother refused to have anything to do with it. She didn't think I should be getting married in a church, not even a little storefront church, and certainly not in a white wedding dress. Richard's mother and aunt insisted that I wear one since this was his first marriage. It was a big wedding dress—way too big for me—that they had bought at the Goodwill. My ring came from Woolworth's, a solitaire-cut piece of glass set in a metal that turned my finger green.

Richard and I stayed together only a few months. I left him after he tried to beat me up one day. I never saw him again. When I filed for divorce in 1969, he was living at the Jackson State Prison, a maximum security facility in Jackson, Michigan.

After I returned with my children to my parents' house, I went to work as a chamber maid at the Sheraton Cadillac Hotel in downtown Detroit, a few blocks from the Patton Parking Garage where my father parked cars. I worked an afternoon shift. My sister helped take care of my children while I was at work. In those days racism ran rampant in most places in the city and particularly those that catered to the white middle and upper classes. Black people rarely entered the Sheraton Cadillac unless they were employees or celebrities like Jackie Robinson, who autographed a cocktail napkin for me.

I was part of the housekeeping staff, but I didn't clean hotel rooms. The personnel director who hired me felt that I was too young to be assigned to the rooms. Instead, I walked around all day in a black maid's uniform, complete with little white apron and cap, and a little broom and dust pan. I swept up dirt and cigarette butts, emptied ashtrays and wiped down the chairs in the ballrooms and main lobbies. As one of the youngest girls on the staff, I got lots of advice and encouragement from the other black employees. They often lectured me about the importance of going back to school. I especially liked the banquet waiters and waitresses. They looked so professional in their black uniforms. They provided elegant table service for some of the city's most exclusive social events. And they took great pride in their work. I wanted to be like them.

After about a year of walking around cleaning dirty ashtrays, I went to the personnel director and asked her if I could be a banquet waitress. She told me that I had to be a busgirl first and that as soon as an opening came up in one of the dining rooms, she would have me transferred. I now had a plan, a goal to achieve that would enable me to better support my children. But I got pregnant again. Rather than wait until I was fired—pregnant women on the housekeeping staff were regularly "let go"—I quit my maid's job. I managed to keep my pregnancy from my parents long enough to apply for public assistance and move to a small attic apartment on the East Side, about two miles from my parents' house. Whenever my mother visited, I put on a big muu-muu or tent dress so she couldn't see my expanding belly.

One day when I was expecting the welfare caseworker, I answered the doorbell wearing the only maternity dress I owned. There stood my mother. She looked at my big belly and turned around and left. I was nineteen when I gave birth to my youngest daughter on June 24, 1965. I no longer feared that my children would be taken from me since I was now legally married, but I had disgraced my family again, not only by having another child, but by becoming a breeding black welfare mother.

Welfare is an entitlement. It was established in 1935 as part of the Social Security Act to ensure that single (white) widowed women with young children who were in need of financial support got it. The idea was that these women needed to be at home taking care of their kids and should be compensated for their care giving. That all changed when black women began applying in large numbers for assistance. Suddenly the discourse of welfare and its policies changed from socially sanctioned benevolence for the best interest of children to the vilification of black unwed mothers, even though 60 percent of welfare recipients were white women in 1965. Of course, I didn't know all this when I first stepped into a welfare office, pregnant and with my two young children, to ask for help.

Applying for welfare certainly didn't seem like something I was entitled to. The mainly white social workers I encountered during the years I received welfare and AFDC (Aid to Families with Dependent Children) acted like they had been trained to treat mothers-in-need with as much resentment and hostility as they could muster. Each visit to a welfare office was an assault on what little self-esteem I had left after the ordeal of trying to keep my family together. I made sure my children were clean and well groomed and had something to eat and to occupy them while we spent hours sitting in crowded and dirty rooms waiting to check in with a caseworker.

Not only were the social workers insensitive to me and my children, they further diminished my steadily shrinking sense of dignity by asking all kinds of personal questions. They had the legal right to do so. It also was legal for them to visit—or raid—our houses at any time of the day or night to see if we were hiding a new toaster or television behind the couch or a man under the bed. Although I never had to endure the "midnight raids" the U.S. Supreme Court finally declared unconstitutional in 1967, I had enough white folks dropping by unannounced to snoop around my apartment to motivate me to get off relief as soon as I could. That and the fear I would become apathetic like Lillian and end up with a lot of kids but no job or education.

As it turned out, I didn't have to wait long for my stint on welfare to end. Shortly after my youngest child was born, my landlady said we had to move because her teenage son had complained that the babies were making too much noise and he couldn't sleep. To make matters worse, I allowed the father of my older two children to come back into my life. I let him convince me that he had changed. He swore that he now had a job and wanted us to be a family. He found a nice four-room apartment, took me to pick out some furniture, which he never paid for, and moved us in. Things went well for about two weeks, until I realized that, for someone who had a job, he hardly went anywhere. He slept late just about every day, got up, ate a meal, and then left, saying that he worked the evening shift. The more I asked him about his job, the angrier he got. One night he beat me very badly. I ran out to a nearby phone booth and called the police and my cousin Debbie. By the time the police got there, he was gone. He said that he was going to come back and kill me. I believed him.

When Debbie arrived at the apartment, we packed a few things in bags, gathered up the babies, and went to her house. She ordered me to leave everything else, just walk away. Debbie helped me with the money to rent a little furnished apartment on the East Side, at Holcomb and Forest, where we lived for the next two years. I don't remember all the details, but because of the police report I filed against the children's father, I had to admit to my caseworker that he had been living with us. I was dropped from the welfare program. I took a restraining order out against him so he wouldn't bother me anymore. The only time I saw him was if he happened to be at his mother's house when I brought the children by to visit.

The last time I saw him was shortly before he was murdered in 1974. I had brought the children to see their grandmother, and he was there. I asked him that day, "Why were you always beating on me? Do you hate me?" He said he didn't know but that he had always loved me. He was shot to death in front of a pool hall after getting into a fight with another man. He died from a gunshot wound to the chest.

◆ ◆ ◆

Within weeks after I was dropped from welfare, I went back to work at the Sheraton Cadillac Hotel, this time as a busgirl in the main dining room. The wages were poor. We relied mainly on tips, which were quite good at that time. Finally things were becoming a bit more stable in my life. The apartment wasn't much, but I kept it clean. I kept my children clean and well fed. I tried to be a model mother. I was determined to beat the odds, to work my way up to banquet waitress and save my money and buy a house and put my children through school like many of the black banquet waiters and waitresses whom I admired had done.

There was one big problem, though—I didn't have adequate and reliable child care. I couldn't afford it. I worked an afternoon shift, from 2 to 10 p.m. I relied on my neighbor Gloria to keep the children while I was at work. We lived in adjoining apartments separated by a hallway. Gloria would bring the children into her apartment until bedtime, after which she put them to bed and left both apartment doors open. That way she could check in on my sleeping babies until I got home, usually around 11 p.m. That was the best I could do in terms of child care. She took care of my children, and I took care of hers on my days off.

For some reason I no longer remember, one day Gloria was unable to keep the children. I had to get to work. I couldn't afford to take a day off, not only because I would lose pay; I could lose my job since I had already missed days to stay home with my children when they were sick. I asked a neighbor if she would let her fifteen-year-old daughter keep the children. This neighbor had ten children, including two who were around the age of my older children, about three and four. What I didn't know until much later was that the woman also had a serious heroin addiction. In fact, she died of a heroin overdose a few years after I left the East Side. Anyway, the woman told me that she had to attend a funeral and that her daughter had to stay home and watch the younger children.

We arranged for the girl to bring the children to my apartment and stay there until the woman got back home. She assured me that she would come back right after the funeral. She didn't return until much later that night. When I got back from work, the girl was sitting in the apartment with my children, coloring in a coloring book. The baby was in her crib crying. She smelled as if she had been wearing a soiled diaper all day. When I asked the girl about her mother, she said that she didn't know what time she came back but that she had taken her little brother and sister home. She also didn't know why my baby was crying. I picked the child up. She was cold and nasty from the dirty diaper.

I sent the girl home and got the baby ready for a bath. I put her in the tub and started filling it with warm water to wash off the shit that by this time had caked on her little body. Every time I wrung some water from the washrag down her back, she screamed and shivered. When I got her cleaned up, I saw that her body had bruises all over it. I grabbed the baby up, wrapped her in a blanket, and found someone to take me to Detroit Receiving Hospital. I didn't wait to try and find out what had happened to my baby. She was badly hurt and needed immediate medical attention.

The response of the hospital staff was fierce. A nurse took the baby to an examination room. She was examined by a doctor and then all hell broke loose, mainly because I couldn't tell them what had happened. I told the doctor that I had just gotten home from work and that's how I found her. He yelled at me, "Then why didn't you call the police?" I answered, "Because I don't have a telephone. It was quicker for me to get somebody to bring her here than to go around finding somebody at home who had a telephone." He didn't believe me. Neither did any of the nurses who attended to my baby. They kept asking me, "How did this happen?" I didn't know. The doctor asked, "What kind of mother are you? This baby has been beaten and you don't know what happened? You didn't even bother to find out?"

I kept trying to tell him that my only concern was getting her to the hospital right away. My baby was hurt. The only thing on my mind was getting her to a doctor. I didn't have time to ask the babysitter and her mother what happened. I said that I would find out when I got back home. He said, "If I had my way, you won't be going home. You would be going straight to jail." I kept saying over and over again, "I didn't beat my baby. I just got home from work. You can call the Sheraton Cadillac Hotel. They can tell you exactly what time I got there and what time I left. I take the bus. It takes me forty-five minutes to get home. You can see that I didn't waste any time getting her to the hospital. I didn't beat my baby."

They wanted to know about my other children. I told them that they were home alone and that I didn't have time to find someone to keep them. This made the doctor and nurses even more angry. It didn't matter that I didn't have anyone to watch the children. As far as they were concerned, I was unfit to have children and they told me so.

It was early morning when I left the hospital. They kept my baby. I went straight to the babysitter's house and told her mother that somebody had beaten my baby and I wanted to know what happened and why she didn't come back from the funeral like she said she would. All I could find out from them is that the girl left the apartment for a few minutes. When she came back, my baby was crying and she didn't know why, so she put her in her crib and left her there. I later learned from my other children that the girl put my baby in her potty chair before she left the apartment and was gone for a long time. The two other children—the girl's siblings—beat and bit my baby while she was locked in the chair. My children were too young to do anything to protect their sister, but they finally got them to stop.

The girl and her mother denied any wrongdoing. A neighbor later told me that they didn't want the police investigating them, so they lied and said that I was always sleeping around with different men and one of them beat my baby. My mother even bought into the lie and accused me of being an unfit mother. The only support I received was from Gloria, a Nation of Islam couple who lived across the street from me, and my cousin Debbie. They all knew those people were lying and that I was doing my best to care for my children. In fact, I was one of the few women in the neighborhood who worked outside the home. Everyone else was either on welfare or had husbands or boyfriends who supported them.

My baby was in the hospital for more than a week while I was being investigated. I went to visit her every day but couldn't stay long. That added fuel to the flame of accusations surrounding us. Nobody, not even the social worker whom I was required to meet with *before* I was allowed to visit my baby, took into consideration that I couldn't spend the day with her like the other mothers who had children in the pediatrics ward, because I had to go to work. I had two other children to support. I would sit in the social worker's office and stare straight ahead while she asked, "What are you thinking about, Sandra?" My usual response was, "I'm thinking about how I'd like to go see my baby now. While I'm sitting here with you, I could be with my baby. I have to go to work in a little while, and you're making me sit here. I want to see my baby now." Every day, the same routine. That woman taking up time I could be spending with my baby, asking me the same question, "What are your thinking, Sandra." Like I was going to tell her. *Tune-out time.*

My daughter's crib was at the far end of the ward. Whenever she saw me come in, she would bounce up and down and laugh and hold her little arms out for me to pick her up. Walking the gauntlet of angry and hostile mothers was difficult. They never spoke to me; they just watched silently as I passed by them, my eyes straight ahead to where my baby waited for me to come and hold her. It was the same with the doctors and nurses who were on duty when I arrived. They stared. I knew what they were thinking and saying behind my back. "There she is, the one who beat her baby. She comes in here for a few minutes and then leaves. She doesn't even stay to feed her baby." My mother had visited my baby and told me what the other mothers were saying about me. Nobody wanted to take into account that I couldn't stay because I had to go to work.

A few days after I brought my baby home from the hospital, a social worker came to visit, a handsome young black man fresh out of Wayne State University's School of Social Work. He was the first black social worker I had ever met. He was kind. He said he was surprised by how neat and clean my apartment was. And he looked everywhere, in the bedrooms, in the bathroom and the tiny kitchen. I told him that my mother had always taught her children that no matter how little you have, you must be neat and clean.

I guess people expect that being poor means having a dirty house. I took care of what I had. And I didn't have much. Just an old easy chair in the living room, an old table with three chairs in the tiny kitchen, a really old stove that I wish I had kept—it would be an expensive antique today—and an old bed in each of the bedrooms. The apartment was already furnished when I rented it. It was dreary, though, so I bought some paint and painted it a bright yellow to make it cheery.

The young social worker played with my children for a few minutes. Then we went into the kitchen where he laid out some forms for me to sign. He said, "We've reviewed your case and, frankly, we don't know how you're living on what you earn. We're going to help you out. We're going to give you some food stamps and a stipend for child care."

He helped me with the forms and explained what I was *entitled* to as a single mother applying for public aid. He gave me the names of dentists and family doctors in the area who accepted Medicaid and encouraged me to take advantage of their medical services, which I did. He also asked me about my plans for the future. I told him that I wanted to be a banquet waitress because they made good money and only worked about twenty-five hours a week. That way, I could spend more time with my children. He thought it was a good idea, offered more words of encouragement, and left. Things were going to ease up a bit for me now. But I still needed to find a responsible person to care for my children while I worked. My cousin Debbie wanted to help by adopting my youngest child.

Debbie was ten years older than I, had a stable relationship with a man who worked every day, a neat little house not far from my apartment, and no children. She regularly came around to see about mine. Each time she visited she asked me to give her my baby. "Sandy, let me take her. This thing wouldn't have happened if you'd let me have her. Let me take her home. You can come and see her whenever you want." I refused. I hadn't gone through the ordeal of keeping my family together to separate us now. I was determined to keep my children together. I eventually sent my younger daughter to live with Debbie for a while after she returned to Kentucky, where my mother's relatives still live. My baby was about eight years old then. She regularly wrote me letters telling me how much she loved living in the country. "Can I stay, Mommie? Please let me stay." And I did, until I couldn't bear to be separated from her any longer.

◆ ◆ ◆

We lived on Holcomb near Forest until after the riots of 1967 practically destroyed the neighborhood. I found a larger place on Garland and Mack, right across the street from Cantrell's Funeral Home. It was a four-family flat. The woman across the hall from me agreed to babysit. She had three or four teenage children and was home all day, so I thought it would be safe to leave my children with her, especially since I could now pay for child care. I was wrong. The woman spent her entire day in front of the television watching the soaps rather than my children. To make matters worse, her kids set me up several times to be robbed. I got robbed so many times that I stopped buying things for my house. Twice I bought a television set, only to leave with my children for the day and come back to find the place burglarized.

The last time it happened was the final straw. Someone broke in while my children were in the bedroom asleep and my babysitter was in her apartment across the hall watching television. They busted up the big piggy bank I kept for the kids and took all the pennies—*pennies!* They also took a sewing machine I had recently bought. That made me really mad. I found out that a couple of dopeheads who lived downstairs had done it, so I called the cops and had them arrested. When I went to court, they tried to intimidate me by glaring in my direction, but the judge was sympathetic. I don't remember how much time they got, but they went to jail.

Debbie's boyfriend came over a few days after I was robbed and gave me a gun, a derringer, and instructed me how to use it. "Now, all you gotta do is hold the gun like this, make sure the safety lock is off, and the next time somebody kicks your door in, blow they asses away." He stood in the doorway and told me to point the gun at him but not to shoot him, so I could get an idea of where to aim. "Wait 'til he steps in the house. Don't shoot him while he's out here in the hallway. You don't want nobody charging you with murder for shootin' this motherfucker. And aim for the heart! Aim for the heart! Now, when you shoot him, he's probably going to fall backwards, so you gonna have to pull him into the house. Make sure he's in the house before you call the cops."

Fortunately, I never had to put this plan into action. A friend named Ted offered a safer solution. When I told him about the break-ins, he said, "Y'all not safe here. Y'all need to come and live with me. I got a big house over on Hazelwood."

Ted had gone to high school with my older brother and sister. He grew up a block away from my parents' house and had been a family friend for years. He and his wife had recently separated and Ted was lonely. We moved in; within weeks Ted and I were a couple. We lived together for about four years during which Ted became the only real father figure my children ever had. However, our relationship began to fall apart when he refused to marry me. He would often say, "I'll live with you forever, but we're not getting married."

The other thing that put a strain on our relationship was my enrollment in 1971 in a G.E.D. program. It was called Operation Second Chance. My friend Gladys found out about the program while working as an aide at Hutchins Middle School, right across the street from where we lived. She and another neighbor were the first in our group of mothers to go.

One day they stopped by my house and tried to get me to enroll. Gladys said, "You read all the time, so you might as well go and get your G.E.D." I wasn't interested.

By that time I had achieved my goal of becoming a banquet waitress. I had also been promoted to waitress for the lunch hour in the Motor Bar at the Sheraton Cadillac Hotel. I had good working hours. I reported to work at 10 a.m. and was done at 4 p.m. I had plenty of time to get the two older children ready for school and the younger one next door to the babysitter, an elderly woman who took very good care of my child. I was back home in time to get dinner ready. On weekends I worked the lineup, that is, I was sent out with a team of waiters and waitresses to serve banquets and private parties. I usually started around 5:30 p.m. and was done by about 9:30.

When I wasn't at my jobs, I was working in the house, cooking, cleaning, doing laundry, sewing, proving that I was a good mother. I took my children on outings every chance I got. We went to the library, the zoo, Belle Isle, anywhere we could get to by bus since I didn't have a car. I also started a savings account. A sense of stability had finally settled on me, so much so that after Gladys kept encouraging me to go to Operation Second Chance, I said okay. After all, I had nothing to lose.

I signed up and within three months the instructors told me that I could take the test at any time. I took the G.E.D. exam in April of 1971 and got such high scores that the counselors and instructors at Operation Second Chance cheered when I reported to their office. I was a bit stunned by their excitement. The director of the program said to me, "You don't know what you've done, do you?" I didn't. He smiled and said, "You just went over to the testing center and showed everybody what a black girl can do with the G.E.D!"

I was surprised and relieved. I knew I had done well. It was a five-part exam and took two days to complete. On the second day the man who was monitoring the exam stopped by my desk and whispered, "We've graded the first three parts. You're doing great. Keep it up." I asked him, "Is it good enough for me to get into college?" He said, "Yes. Just about any four-year college in the country, and you're not even finished yet. Keep up the good work."

When I met with my instructors afterward, I asked again, "Is this good enough for me to get into college? Can you go to college if you never went to high school?" They explained that the G.E.D., the General Education Development certificate, is equivalent to a high school diploma. I sat there in a daze as my counselor called Wayne State University and made an appointment for me to meet with an admissions counselor. I couldn't believe it. I was going to college after all. I was the first person in my family to attend college.

◆ ◆ ◆

I enrolled at Wayne State University in June of 1971. I earned a Bachelor of Arts degree with a double major in French and English and a secondary teaching certificate. But it wasn't easy. Here I was, a twenty-four-year-old black woman with three children starting out as a freshman with few skills beyond being an avid reader and good writer. I had no idea how to take notes and prepare for exams. I didn't even know how to study. Everything was a tremendous effort. Furthermore, my relationship with Ted was falling apart. The more I immersed myself in my studies, the more attention he demanded from me.

I knew after my first year of college that it was time to leave Ted. I had saved some money and, with the advice and guidance of one of the young black businessmen who, by 1970, had begun to patronize the Motor Bar in the Sheraton Cadillac Hotel where I worked, I bought a house on the West Side. I also went to my AFDC caseworker and proposed that I be allowed to collect full benefits for four years rather than the stipend I had been receiving. I did some simple calculations and showed her how much money it would cost the state to continue supplementing my income until my youngest child turned eighteen. I then showed her how much the state would save if I could earn a bachelor's degree in four years and go to work full time. I knew nothing about inflation and cost-of-living increases. I just multiplied what I was receiving by X number of years.

This caseworker was a black woman. She listened quietly and said that she would see what she could do. I don't know how she managed it, but her adroit manipulation of the levers of bureaucracy enabled me to quit the waitress job so that I could study full time. She later told me that I had impressed her with my eagerness to pursue this goal and my efforts to make a convincing argument in economic terms. I went to school every semester, including summers, and finished in four and a half years. I taught as a substitute for a while, then, in the fall of 1976, a former French teacher recommended me for a job as an academic adviser in the College of Liberal Arts at Wayne State University.

This was a major break for me. Now I was in an intellectual community, and the university offered excellent benefits, including a tuition reimbursement for any employee who completed a course with a grade of C or better. As soon as I received my first paycheck, I called my social worker and thanked her and told her that I no longer needed public assistance. It felt good, even though my salary put me just above the poverty level. With a good health care plan for me and my children and free tuition for continued study, I knew I could make it. A door of opportunity had been opened for me, and I walked right in.

For the next seven years I took one course a semester toward a master's degree in French. I worked night and day to put my three children through parochial high school. I got up at 4:30 each morning and delivered the *Wall Street Journal*, returned home to get the kids up and ready for school and myself ready for work at the university. I taught adult education classes two nights a week. The rest of the time I spent with my children. It was time well spent. My two oldest children are college graduates; my youngest completed her junior year of college and decided to go into the corporate world, where she has carved out a successful and lucrative career for herself.

Among my regrets, and I have many, is that I had to leave my youngest child behind when, in 1983, I left Detroit to pursue a Ph.D. in Comparative Literature at the University of Wisconsin—Madison. I did so on the advice of my parents. The struggle had taken its toll. By that time I had become very depressed, severely anorexic, and was drinking way too much.

My father came to my house one day during an especially dark period for me. My two older children had gone away to college. All I had left was the youngest one. She was a teenager. She didn't want to be hanging out with her mother, and she let me know it. I had devoted my life to my children and now I felt terribly alone.

My father told me that he was proud of me. He said, "You changed your whole life, and you did it with your mind. But your children are killing you. You just about worked yourself to death trying to support them and put them through school. You got an opportunity to get your Ph.D., and you should do it. Go on to Wisconsin and leave my granddaughter here. Your mother and I will look after her." I completed my doctoral degree in June of 1989, and started teaching in the Department of Afro-American Studies that fall.

PART TWO

CHAPTER 6

Madison, Wisconsin

From the moment I stepped off the plane in 1983, I knew that Madison, Wisconsin, would be my permanent home. It's my refuge from the ugliness of Detroit, the city of my birth. But it's not the easiest place to be in terms of meaningful social interactions outside the university community. I knew before I got here that Madison wouldn't offer much in terms of a social life, but that was okay. I had come to immerse myself in literature and to become a university professor.

I achieved my goals long ago, but I never felt that I quite fit into university culture. There was something missing, a certain *joie de vivre*, that I wanted to experience but couldn't. Perhaps it's because academics take themselves too seriously. They don't know how to play. By the time I reached the rank of full professor, that is exactly what I wanted to do—play.

I found my playground in 1999, in the theater. Now, after years of hard work and study and the solitude of writing dense, academic books and articles that few people read, I was retraining myself, redefining myself as an actor. It has not been easy, especially at my age, to put myself out there, to take risks with the emotional palette that is the actor's tool, to experience the vulnerability that actors live with, to deal with rejection as part of the job, to feel my confidence diminish during rehearsals as it becomes apparent to everyone watching, especially the director, that the talent is there but my skills are woefully lacking. I have now reached professional status. I've earned the coveted Actors' Equity card, but I am still learning my craft. This new path is not easy, but the reward of creating something with others is worth the risks that theater demands.

I once mentioned to my colleague, Michael Thornton, that I'm sure my anxiety about winning all that money in the casino had to do with my background as a member of the black underclass and my belief that you work for what you get, that hard work has its own rewards. He laughed and said, "It's a good thing you didn't win the lottery." I thought about that. Winning the lottery would be like a fairy godmother's dropping a load of money on me. It would be pure chance, since I don't think I've bought more than three or four lottery tickets in my life. And when I did, I forgot I had them. I never even bothered to look in the paper for the winning numbers or watch the television shows where they pull the winning numbers. It was too much trouble. Buying lottery tickets never felt like gambling to me. They were something I picked up at the grocery store, something I bought on a whim because I suddenly felt lucky.

No, this was something else. This was GAMBLING. But it didn't demand anything of me, not like poker or blackjack—games that require you to think a little bit or, at the very least, to pay attention to what's going on around you. All I have to do is sit in front of a machine, put money in, press the Bet Max button and maybe I'll get some money back.

Whatever was happening to me had as much to do with the machines as with my steadily decreasing powers of choice, my will power. The machines beckon you, even when there's nobody in front of them. The "Wheel of Fortune" machines are the worst. In fact, I'd begun to find them downright offensive: they wouldn't give me any money, and they never stopped making a racket. Their recorded chorus hollers, "Wheel of Fortune!!!" every few seconds, it seems, even when nobody's around. Sometimes I felt like shouting, "WILL SOMEBODY COME AND TURN THESE DAMN THINGS OFF?"

Then there's the "Marilyn Monroe" machine. The voice impersonating Marilyn says, "Come on, let's play." She sings, "I want to be loved by you, but you alone." She impersonates Betty Boop with a sultry "Boop Boop a Doo." And when you win, as I once did during a visit to Ho Chunk, she says, "Hey, you're on a roll! Congratulations! Come, let's play!", encouraging you to put more money in the machine. I was tempted that day, but I hit the Cash Out button, redeemed my ticket, and folded two crisp new hundred-dollar bills into my fanny pack. I had every intention of leaving right away, but after having a little luck with Marilyn, I decided to try Betty Boop on my way out. The little Betty Boops teased me by lighting up every now and then, but not once did I hear them say, "Boop Boop a Doo," not too much to ask considering the amount of money I was paying them.

On top of the machine, or, rather, the carousel of twelve linked "Betty Boop" machines, is a digital monitor flashing the value of the jackpot that grows with each quarter players drop into the slots. It was well over $235,000 when I left Ho Chunk that day, feeling despondent after letting Betty Boop trick me out of the hundred-dollar bills I had so carefully stored away in my fanny pack. I wondered what lucky person would come in and play and leave rich, thanks to the willingness of hundreds of other people to subsidize his or her good fortune.

By mid-July of 2005, I had begun to wonder about a lot of things and to seek answers. Like whether the voice-over work behind Marilyn's and Betty's come-ons is covered by the American Federation of Television and Radio Artists. (It is, according to the fall, 2006 edition of the *AFTRA Newsletter.*) I wondered what kinds of residuals are paid to the estates of Elvis and Lucille Ball for the use of the ten-second video clips from their performances and shows that slot players pay to watch. I also wondered whether the sick feeling I experienced whenever I entered the casinos was the result of being over stimulated. Too many sounds, too many blinking lights, too much darkness. And way too many slot machines. Rows and rows of slot machines.

I remember that, after I won the $6,000 jackpot, I whispered to the woman who brought me my check that I'm really not a gambler. She said, "Well, then, be careful. This can be very seductive, and remember that the casino is set up to win."

I had already been seduced. Seduced by the possibility of winning more money and bigger jackpots. Seduced by a fantasy—that I had become Queen of the Slot Machines. Just as Michael Thornton had predicted when I stopped by his office to tell him about my gambling, I went from being so sure that my completely irrational behavior the previous week—going to Ho Chunk and deliberately losing $900— had cured me of my sudden and intense urge to gamble to deciding, quite impulsively, to return and try to recoup the loss.

◆ ◆ ◆

What precipitated this turnabout? A literal turnabout. It happened on Sunday, June 19, 2005, a warm and sunny Sunday afternoon, a stay-at-home day. I got up early, made myself a hot and foamy double cappuccino, listened to Musica Antigua on the radio, and read the *New York Times*, my Sunday leisure activity. I did my stretches and warm-ups and started out on a five-mile jog along Lake Mendota Drive. Suddenly, the idea that I would win lots of money if I went back to Ho Chunk, maybe another $6,000 jackpot, took over. I turned around and jogged home, changed clothes, and headed to the casino.

For some strange reason I decided when I got there that I needed sunglasses inside the casino. By this time I'd abandoned my Bucky Badger T-shirt and jeans and baseball cap for the summer skirts and dresses I prefer. Cotton and washable silk, because my clothes stink when I leave the casino and have to be washed. *I* stink when I leave the casino from all the cigar and cigarette smoke and the general funky odors that seem to go with gambling. I wore a simple light blue cotton sundress and dark sunglasses—a sunglass clip, really. Not exactly ghetto fabulous but a great deal better than the way the general casino clientele dresses.

I made my entrance and looked around for a few seconds before heading to the bar to buy a Heineken. The Queen had arrived, but nobody noticed. Not at first. Everybody was too busy looking at their machines. The bartender recognized me, greeting me with "Hello, Princess. You look lovely." He gave me the Heineken and wished me good luck.

As I walked around the casino drinking my beer and looking at the people sitting at their machines, I suddenly felt self-conscious. There's nothing glamorous about gambling in casinos in the Midwest. Truth be told, there's something pathetic about all the sloppily dressed, heavily smoking, silver-haired women and men digging deep into their purses, wallets, and pockets, looking for money to buy a few more spins, to keep the jackpot hope alive for just a few more minutes. Casinos in the U.S. have no formal dress code, so people come as they are: the men in rumpled shirts and jeans, their bellies hanging way too far over their belts; the women haggard-looking in tan khakis or wide-butt bermuda shorts. And everybody sucking on cigarettes.

Ho Chunk Casino is in Sauk County, near the Wisconsin Dells tourist resorts, too far from urban areas to attract black people. I stood out, even when I wasn't decked out as I was that Sunday. Rarely did I see more than five or six other black people. I spoke to a couple of the black women I saw there that day. One said that she and her husband were from Milwaukee. I asked if they went to Potawatomi. "No," she said. "We don't like to gamble that close to home, so every now and then we come here, get a room at the hotel, and stay for the weekend."

Another woman said that she and her husband live in Illinois but have a summer home in Fond Du Lac and that she's always surprised to see other black people at the casino. If they look friendly, as she said I did, she'll chat with them, find out where they're from. But usually when I was there, the casino was filled with elderly white people, senior citizens. They pump millions of dollars into Ho Chunk Casino. They arrive by the busloads. They enter in wheelchairs and leaning on walkers and, sometimes, pulling an oxygen tank along behind them.

The Sunday I decided to arrive incognito in my blue sundress and dark sunglasses was the first time I saw someone in the casino with an oxygen tank. I was truly bewildered. I wanted to ask him, "Why come to a place that's detrimental to your health when you're already suffering from emphysema or some other deadly respiratory disease?"

Of course, I didn't ask. I pretended not to notice, but it troubled me, not only because of the health hazard to the man but also, isn't oxygen highly flammable? All those people lighting up cigars and cigarettes, apparently oblivious to a man walking around with an oxygen tank. We could all go up in smoke.

It still troubles me to see so many elderly and ill people sitting in casinos, staring at their slot machines, when they need to be getting some fresh air or going for a walk or engaging in some sort of physical or mental exercise, like playing Scrabble. They come because they're bored. For those living in nursing homes and senior citizen communities, going to casinos is an outing, an organized social activity that breaks up the monotony of their daily existence.

As I made my round of the casino floor, still wearing my sunglass clip and pretending to be doing research for a book about gambling (a lie—I was not writing a book at that time; I just said that to make myself seem better than everybody else), I struck up a conversation with an elderly lady who was sticking quarters into a Betty Boop machine. She told me that coming to the casino is an adventure. It gives her something to do. And the employees treat her very well, offering her free coffee and sodas, and even watching her machine when she has to go to the ladies' room. She even earns points on her rewards card and has won a couple of good meals there.

I didn't realize until she mentioned it that many of the slot players were tethered to their machines by a long cord attached to their shirts or blouses. At the end of the cord was a rewards card which they inserted into the machine. The more you play, the more points you earn toward a complimentary meal, room at the hotel, or merchandise, such as an umbrella or flashlight or mini-calculator or other useless junk. One thing is certain: by 2005, when I first stepped into a casino to play the slots, gambling among older adults had increased dramatically, the result of the rapid expansion of casinos throughout the country, marketing directors' savvy targeting of the elderly, and the casino employees who make seniors feel very, very, welcome. Casino gambling was helping them fill a void; perhaps it was filling a void for me too, although I couldn't recognize it as such back then.

Considering that most of Ho Chunk's gamblers are white and middle-aged and beyond, this would be poetic justice if it wasn't so pathetic. Like that of other Native American tribes, the history of the Ho Chunk is one of treaties made and broken by the U.S. government, resulting in their losing millions of acres; of brutal and forced removals from their homelands; of familial disruptions in the interest of educating young native children in the "American way;" of racism and disenfranchisement; of poverty stemming from several centuries of mistreatment by white people.

That was one of the reasons I felt so self-conscious that Sunday afternoon when I decided to pretend to be a writer. Given my own experiences with poverty, the kind of excessiveness in which I was engaging was inexcusable, especially since I got no pleasure out of it and certainly was not lacking in more meaningful and less expensive things to do. This was not entertainment for me, no matter how much the advertisers promote it as such. By the looks of the other people moving like zombies from one machine to another trying to get a hit, some complaining about how the casino was acting like it didn't want to pay anybody anything, it wasn't entertaining for them, either. They weren't having fun. They were there for the money. So was I. Although I had all I needed to make it through September, I wanted more. I wanted to win again. But, as everyone who gambles knows, if you keep it up, you're bound to lose. And I lost that day.

At that time I didn't have an ATM card and had never bothered to get a PIN number for my credit card because I never wanted to have such easy access to my bank accounts. So I paid a 6.5 percent fee for the privilege of cashing a $300 personal check at the casino and joined the other slot players buzzing from one machine to another, hoping each time that this would be the lucky one. Since I couldn't see very well with my dark sunglass clip on, I took it off and put it in my dress pocket. Less than forty-five minutes after I stopped pretending to be a writer and started stuffing $20 bills into the machines, I'd lost the money. I left the casino feeling sick. Not only had I lost $300; I also lost the $65 sunglass clip. Not to mention the gas I'd wasted. By then it was at $1.89 a gallon and climbing. My unhappy Sunday excursion had cost me almost $400. That was it. The casino was not where I wanted to spend my time. I was never going back.

◆ ◆ ◆

No matter how many times I swore that I was done with gambling, something would draw me back. This time I was back less than a week later. I began thinking about going to the casino as soon as I got a call from the Wehmann Talent Agency to ask if I could come to Minneapolis for a print audition for Slumberland. That night I could hardly sleep. I woke up the next morning at around five. I tried to lie in bed and rest but couldn't. Minneapolis is a four-hour ride from Madison and I planned to drive over and right back.

Before I left, I withdrew $300 from my checking account, so I could stop and play the slots. This time I went to two casinos belonging to the Ho Chunk Nation. I'd looked them up on the Internet before I went to bed. On the way back to Madison I stopped at the Majestic Pines Casino in Black River Falls. I immediately lost $300 on the gold bar machine. I stayed at that machine because I'd won $2,000 on one like it at Ho Chunk Casino a couple of weeks earlier.

Why didn't I try some of the other ones instead? Didn't I know by then that one jackpot doesn't mean the same machine in a different casino is going to spit out another? I left Majestic Pines and went straight to Ho Chunk, where I took a $300 advance on my credit card. I'd only ever done that once and then I was gambling. Now I'd done it again. I lost most of it, won it back, then lost it again. This is what casinos expect, that people who win, especially those who win big, will keep coming back to win more and finally lose what they'd won. What a vicious circle!

That's what was happening with me. I kept telling myself that if I didn't stop, I would lose what was supposed to be my summer support. For someone who for years had tried to be careful with money and save, save, save, I felt surprisingly calm that night, despite my losses, which that week alone totaled $900. Maybe my calmness had something to do with not having earned that money. I'd won it by feeding slot machines. Inside the casino money is devalued. Gamblers trade their everyday concern about the value of money, what it can buy in tangible goods and services, for what it might bring: a jackpot. Money also changes ownership. We think of the money we win as not really our money but rather the casino's money, even though it's in our hand or pocket or purse.

By this time I wasn't winning so much as cycling money in and out of my bank account. I never was able to think in terms of being up or down or breaking even, the way I would hear some of the other people talking. One day a woman at the machine next to me smiled sadly and said, to no one in particular, "Well, if I break even, I'm satisfied. It's fun, after all." She wasn't very convincing as she sighed and took a long draw on her cigarette and blew her smoke my way. My thought, as it always was when I went to the casino, was, "You really shouldn't be here. You can't afford to keep losing $300 every time you come here, no matter how that money got into your bank account."

Sometimes I won, doubling or tripling the initial $300. In two months—between April 30, 2005, when I won $1,180 at Ho Chunk, and June 30, 2005—I had wagered and lost $2,606 against total winnings of $12,100. Any normal person would consider herself lucky to have won nearly 1.5 times what she would've earned by teaching an intensive summer course. But no, I wanted more, so I devised a plan. If I was going to gamble, I needed to set up a separate bank account to keep my gambling bankroll separate from my other money, and get an ATM card, and use it only at the bank's ATMs so I would stop leaving a paper trail all over the place. And I would always keep $300 in cash at the house, in case of a sudden casino attack. That way I would avoid the fees for cashing checks or for cash advances.

Fortunately, I got cast in a play and spent most of the first two weeks of July 2005, traveling back and forth to Beloit, Wisconsin. By the time I'd get home to Madison, I was too tired to go to the casino, so the gambling slowed down somewhat.

◆ ◆ ◆

The play was called *Imprints: The Beloit Ghost Stories Project* and was based on ghost stories the director, Amy Sarnos, had collected from some of the town's older residents. Each story was a history lesson about some of the more eccentric people who lived there, died there, and now return to haunt people.

The stories about how black folks ended up in Beloit were particularly interesting, another episode in the Great Migration of the late 1800s and early 1900s, when blacks left the South in droves. Promised new homes and good wages, they came to Beloit to work at the Fairbanks-Morse factory, making engines for ships. Learning their history made me appreciate even more the struggles my people have had to overcome just to survive. The Eastern European immigrants who also came got new homes; the black people didn't. And although their wages were better than what they earned in the South, they were given the most dangerous and nasty jobs. The same story played out all over the industrializing North. The promises, the lies.

The *Beloit Ghost Stories Project* was hardly high drama, but it offered me a much needed opportunity to gain more experience onstage. We were a cast of seven, including Josh Burton, who founded New Court Theatre at Beloit College in 2000. The two younger actors—fresh out of acting school—made it clear by their behavior during the first week that they weren't going to be team players. Wannabe stars, that's what they were, so I decided to ignore them.

Working on this play was quite an experience, my introduction to what's called community-based theater. We improvised on a script based on oral histories collected from people in the community and used just about anything handy for props. We made theater out of stories and our bodies and not much else.

I spent my fifty-ninth birthday rehearsing or, rather, rolling, sliding, and crawling all over the studio floor with the other actors while Amy stood around beating on a little drum and telling us to move to the rhythms, fill up the space, and to create structures by linking our bodies and limbs together in twos, threes, and so forth. This is always dangerous, because somebody is bound to let out a big fart. You have to be careful where your face ends up, not in somebody's behind, to be sure.

We did these exercises at every rehearsal, sometimes spending thirty or forty minutes rolling around on the floor, getting in touch with our inner selves, I suppose. I was beginning to get worried. When were we going to start putting this show up on its feet? Since Josh and none of the other actors seemed worried, I tried to convince myself that these were bonding exercises intended to make us work as a unit, an ensemble. The problem was that I was running out of ideas for making new shapes. I also worried that I might be the one to let loose with the you-know-what. And I needed to start running my lines and working on developing the characters I was playing: a young woman who had just arrived in Beloit with her husband, a little kid from the black side of town called the "flats," and a ghost hunter.

After rehearsal I got cleaned up and dressed and went to Milwaukee for dinner with a man to whom a friend had introduced me by telephone a few weeks earlier. It was a blind date, the first I'd ever been on in my life. It felt strange to be going to meet someone I knew nothing about except that he liked to travel, enjoyed art and literature, was in his sixties, had been married, and now was single. But it beat spending the rest of the evening of my fifty-ninth birthday alone.

We met at a restaurant because I refused to go to his apartment. He told me during dinner that my refusal to meet at his place had offended him. He said that it wasn't like we'd met on the Internet, so I had nothing to worry about; he meant no harm. I didn't bother to explain or tell him that it was my birthday and this was my way of celebrating, in a restaurant eating good food and enjoying a glass of red wine after spending a hard day at work rolling around on a hardwood floor.

Truth is, I had plenty to worry about. I had wasted a good chunk of my life loving a man who caused me great pain. And now, on my fifty-ninth birthday, I was feeling vulnerable and needed to have some control over this date.

Once we got through his drama, I enjoyed the evening. I left around midnight and headed for Madison thinking that I was battling far too many demons to put any energy into a new relationship, especially with a pot-smoking, cognac-drinking man in his late sixties who didn't seem particularly inclined to engage in any kind of outdoor activities. Like hiking in the Sangre de Cristo Mountains around Taos, New Mexico, or in the sweet-smelling Rio Grande Gorge, or in the beautiful red rocks of Sedona, Arizona. Like we used to do. The poet and me. So many regrets. . . . Nope. I think I'll leave the man from Milwaukee alone.

Heading west on I-94, I passed a billboard for Potawatomi Casino. It was late. I was tired. I wasn't about to end my birthday in a casino. Two exits later I was trying to double back, got lost, and ended up in an unfamiliar neighborhood asking for directions at a "Stop and Go" that must be a favorite hangout for the local thugs. They looked mean. "This is not cool, Adell," I kept telling myself as I got back in my car and drove to the casino. "You don't need to be out here by yourself this time of night asking about a casino. You need to go home." But I went to Potawatomi.

The casino was packed with the most racially and ethnically diverse group of people I had seen in a long time. Especially late at night, casinos in urban areas must be the most multicultural places on the planet. I noticed lots of young people in the casino, mainly at the table games where, if their shouts and groans were any indication, they were having a good time. I watched for a while and then headed for the slots. The slot players were doing what they always do, looking straight at their monitors, oblivious to the activity at the tables. The only difference was that there were fewer elderly people.

I tried a few machines and lost about $100 before winning $1,000 on a Wild Cherry machine. As I watched the monitor register the win, a man walked up behind me, saw what I had won, and said, "Looks like it's time for you to go home." I turned around, looked at him, and agreed. I quickly cashed in my voucher and left. As I walked across the parking lot toward my car, looking back behind me to make sure I wasn't being followed, I again told myself, "Adell, this is not cool, you being out here all by yourself this late at night." I got home around 4:30 a.m. I was exhausted. I tried to sleep, but the noise of the machines kept ringing in my ears. A little voice in my head kept telling me that I should be very, very afraid.

The next morning I stacked my money on the kitchen counter. Occasionally, I would look at my stack of cash and ask myself, "Is this worth the risks you're taking?" The answer was always no. I told my sisters about my latest win and about my increasing anxiety about my too frequent trips to casinos. My sister Brenda reminded me that I might be winning now, but in the long run I would lose so maybe I should stay away for a while. I agreed. Anyway, I needed to focus my time and energy on the play.

Our July 27 opening performance was fast approaching, and we were nowhere near ready. Now, in addition to our human sculpture-building exercises, Amy wanted us to get together and write lyrics and music for the songs that would open each scene. I was surprised by how easy it was, thanks to the more musically inclined members of the ensemble. Once that was done, the stories and bits of history Amy had collected began to come together. It finally was beginning to feel less like work and more like play.

One afternoon, during an open rehearsal, several members of the Southern Wisconsin Paranormal Research Group came to watch. Founded in 1999, the Janesville-based research group is committed to bringing "credibility to the field of paranormal research and to make a concerted effort to display the best evidence and information that is possible." Amy had mentioned the previous day that they would be visiting and that they took their work seriously, so my scene partner—Little Miss Wannabe Star of Stage and Screen—and I were prepared. We were the ghost hunters in the play. Our job was to monitor the paranormal activity that reportedly had been going on for years in the Fairbanks Morse Union Hall. The building was once owned by A. B. Carpenter, a wealthy businessman, devout Congregationalist, and strong opponent of the Fugitive Slave Act, an 1850 Congressional act allowing fugitive slaves to be recaptured, even in non-slaveholding states such as Wisconsin, as part of the Missouri Compromise. Many black residents of Beloit believe the union hall was a station on the Underground Railroad.

The day before the paranormal investigators arrived, Amy gave us some instruments she had borrowed from the research center: a device that looked like a tape recorder and was supposed to measure extreme changes in temperature and another device that records any paranormal activity. Apparently, ghosts create extreme heat or cold to announce their presence. Anyway, according to the Southern Wisconsin Paranormal Research Center's website, these instruments are essential for ghost hunting and are perfect for beginners. My scene partner and I took our work seriously, and aside from a couple of comments about how to correctly hold and read the equipment, the members of the research group (who looked like normal white folks from Wisconsin, by the way), thought we had done a good job of pretending to try to determine whether fugitive slaves were haunting the big union hall that existed onstage only in our imaginations.

Our opening night performance was rough, but by the end of the first week we had gotten our timing down and were beginning to look and feel like an ensemble. It was a good experience, although I could have done without so much floor work. I like ensemble acting and once we were up and running, I began preparing to audition for another ensemble piece, the stage adaptation of Barbara Ehrenreich's best-selling book, *Nickel and Dimed: On (Not) Getting By in America,* which was being produced by the Jewish American Theatre Company in Bloomfield Hills, Michigan, not far from my daughter's house in Orchard Lake.

Ehrenreich went undercover to take unskilled jobs at $6 and $7 an hour and reported on what it's like to try to survive on such meager wages. I had read numerous glowing reviews of the book and wondered what this upper-middle-class white woman with a Ph.D. in biology who wrote for magazines such as *Time, Harper's, The Nation,* and the *New York Times Magazine* could tell me about what I already know: you have to fight like hell to survive on a minimum-wage salary, especially when you are young, black, uneducated and unskilled, single, and have three kids to support. Still, after reading the book, I thought there might be a role for me in the play. After all, Ehrenreich was a tourist among low-wage workers. I had lived for many years the life she reported on.

◆ ◆ ◆

On August 14, 2005, the day after we closed *Imprints,* I headed for Michigan and went on a tour of my own: to just about every casino between Elgin, Illinois, where three days earlier I had won a $2,500 jackpot on the Tiki machine at the Grand Victoria Riverboat Casino (well, $1,700, since I'd wagered $800, although the government would tax me for the $2,500 jackpot as income) and Detroit. I didn't get a role in the play. The Detroit area has plenty of talented black women in my age group who are eager to work for $250 a week, all this small professional theater company was paying at that time. However, *Nickel and Dimed* had made an enormous impression on me. By the time I got to the Blue Chip Riverboat Casino in Michigan City, Indiana, I'd begun to think in economic terms about the people who played the slots and those who worked in casinos. Somewhere in the back of my mind a book was beginning to take shape, a book inspired by *Nickel and Dimed*.

I arrived at the Blue Chip at mid-morning. The place was already jam-packed with people. Some looked like they could hardly afford to be there: women and men desperately in need of good dental plans, extremely overweight people, the elderly, the disabled, the sick. Poor people. I realize that looks can be deceiving, but I have lived long enough among poor people to recognize them. I'm sure that many people I saw in the Blue Chip that day were at the lower end of the socioeconomic ladder—people who could hardly afford to lose their money in this way. Hell, I couldn't have afforded it if I hadn't won it in the first place, and I ain't exactly poor.

What were they risking to be there? What bills weren't getting paid so they could take a chance on the jackpot that would lift them up a few notches above the poverty line? How many were among the estimated forty-seven million Americans who have no health insurance?

And what about the people who work in the casino? Are they employed full time? How many hold down other jobs? What is it like to work in a place where people willingly throw away of millions of dollars a day? These were some of the questions I later tried to find answers for, not by going undercover as Barbara Ehrenreich had done—I would never have made it through an initial screening for a casino job—but by pursuing the route I know best, scholarship, library work. But, first, I had to let this gambling adventure run its course. I had no choice, really, since I was hooked. I just hoped I would soon bring the whole thing to an end without too much damage to my identity, my self-esteem, and my livelihood.

To protect myself once I started working on this book, I tried to use what I had learned from intensive acting training at Shakespeare & Company, one of this country's premier professional acting training programs. I spent a month there, in Lenox, Massachusetts—in the Berkshires—a year earlier, during the summer of 2004, unleashing emotions I'd kept in check for many years under the watchful eyes of the company's founders, Tina Packer and Dennis Krausnick. The actors participating in the program were coached to "allow ourselves to feel" whatever emotions were invoked by the texts we were studying. I worked on the vengeful Queen Margaret in Shakespeare's *Richard III*.

Lots of anger and pain poured out from deep within me into the rehearsal rooms at Shakespeare & Company as I tried to bring out the evil—and humanity—of Shakespeare's hateful queen. Once it started—the anger, the pain—it seemed as if it would never stop. Forty years of closed-off emotion is hard to unleash; it's even harder to accept that it's there, raw material to be accessed for the sake of my art. I survived; I let it happen. I also was letting this gambling experience happen to me, so that I could write about it from the inside, not as a researcher or observer. All I had to do was treat this as an acting experience, go into these spaces—these unreal worlds—and allow myself to feel the emotions.

That's what I kept telling myself, when in fact the book had become an excuse to gamble. Sometimes, as I sat at the slots, my body and mind responding to all the stimuli around and in front of me, I could hear Dennis Krausnick speaking quietly to me: "Allow yourself to feel the emotion, Sandy. But don't lose yourself. You must stay connected to your text and then you'll be okay." The first time I heard his voice was during my first trip to the Blue Chip, on my way to Michigan to audition for *Nickel and Dimed*.

I stayed at the Blue Chip that day long enough to lose $200—about thirty minutes. The tightness of the space (the Blue Chip isn't a riverboat at all; it's a small yacht), the narrow aisles—some of them blocked by wheelchairs and walkers—the intensity of the noise and blinking lights, and the crowds of people making their way from one machine to the next made me sick, literally. I felt like I was going to throw up. I didn't know it at the time, but researchers have found that the labyrinthine layout of casinos and the stress associated with betting and anticipating the outcome—playing with Fate—often produce altered states of consciousness in gamblers.

The sociologist Gerda Reith describes the gambling experience as an adventure or dream state: "When they enter the gambling arena gamblers temporarily step out of the real world, leaving their everyday concerns and routines behind and embarking on an adventure which, as well as being exciting, is also experienced as a state of dream-like dissociation from their surroundings. Their shared feature of separateness means that both gambling games and adventures can assume the properties of dreams, a peculiarity which is caused by the occurrence of the adventure outwith the usual stream of life."

Gamblers become disoriented. The rules and conventions that order the gambler's relation to the everyday world are altered. Logic and reason slip away. The gambler is on sensory overload. According to Dr. Robert Breen, director of the Gambling Treatment Program at Rhode Island Hospital, "When you're sitting in front of that machine, you're intoxicated. You haven't taken a pill, you haven't taken a drink, you haven't put something in your veins. But that doesn't mean that your brain chemistry hasn't changed."

This might explain why I felt dizzy and disoriented as I tried to find my way out of the Blue Chip Casino that day. I hadn't had a drink, but I felt intoxicated. I was relieved to get out into the fresh air and sunshine and away from that boat. I returned to the Blue Chip once, two years later. It had expanded; there was more space between the aisles and more slot machines, including the newly designed, interactive, and even more addictive video slot machines. I experienced the same sickness I had felt when the Blue Chip was a nasty, crowded boat. I was to experience that same sickness every time I entered the labyrinth. But I kept on going.

CHAPTER 7

City of Casinos

As I drove to Michigan from Indiana, I tried to figure out how I had gone from being opposed to casino gambling as a source of revenue for depressed communities like Detroit to participating in this potentially devastating activity. I remember once telling my sister Brenda that Michigan's lawmakers and the Detroit City Council had to be out of their minds if they believed that promoting casino gambling was the way to boost the city's steadily weakening economy and attract tourists to Detroit's blighted downtown and riverfront areas, especially since the Renaissance Center—the $350 million great hope of the 1970s for the city's revitalization—had failed miserably.

For years Michigan residents agreed that this was crazy. They rejected proposals for casinos five times before narrowly approving a referendum in 1996 to open three casinos in Detroit, the MGM Grand and Motor City in 1999, and the Greektown Casino in 2000. But thousands of Michigan residents traveled daily across the waters, to Casino Windsor in Canada, to gamble. Arguments for the economic benefits of casinos on the Detroit side of the Detroit River were too compelling for voters to hold their ground.

Greektown had been a special place for me when I lived in Detroit. It's only about three blocks long, but the coffee houses and bakeries provided me and my children with a glimpse into a culture that was different from ours. Greektown was quaint in those days, the 1970s and early 1980s, when revitalization meant attracting tourists to the Greek restaurants in the area and to the Attic and Detroit Repertory Theaters. It meant turning an old fur trader's warehouse called Trappers Alley into a mall of artists' galleries and specialty shops.

Those memories of Greektown motivated me to go there before heading to my daughter's house in Orchard Lake. I drove downtown to what once had been a familiar and welcoming little community, an escape from my life in Detroit's inner city. It wasn't the same. The Greektown Casino seemed to dwarf everything, at least in my mind. Trappers Alley—my gateway to other cultures—was gone. The brightly lit signs for the casino made everything else irrelevant. The bakeries and restaurants are still there. But the coffee houses and their gatherings of elderly black-clad men have vanished. Now the main attraction is not the food, the belly dancing, or the wonderfully sweet cakes and pastries in the bakeries. Now the real reason to go to Greektown is to gamble.

I felt sad, as if I had lost something precious, as I entered the casino and did my regular routine of walking around trying to look nonchalant, pretending to be cool and not uptight like the other people waltzing from one machine to the next. I later told Brenda that what struck me immediately about this population, aside from its racial and ethnic diversity, was how well dressed some of the people were. I was not accustomed to seeing people in casinos in Armani suits and Anne Klein dresses and carrying Gucci, Louis Vuitton, and Coach handbags. Wisconsinites, especially those who work in universities, are not known for having a sense of style. Give us a pair of khakis, some Birkenstock sandals and white socks, and a shirt or sweater from Land's End, and we think we're looking good.

Brenda told me that the people I saw that afternoon worked in the downtown area, at General Motors' corporate offices, the U.S. Justice Department, and the City-County Building—all within walking distance of the casino. She said that they were probably on their break or lunch hour.

Until then it never occurred to me that people would use their lunch hours and risk getting back to work late for the opportunity to dispose of their money in such an unproductive manner. Although one afternoon, when I was up at Ho Chunk, I saw a hearse in the parking lot and was sure the person driving it had taken a work break to play a few hands of blackjack or play the slots.

It was weird. I walked all around that hearse, which contained a cheap-looking, plain coffin covered by a beige blanket. The backseat held a few plastic wreaths and some little flags. I wondered how the family and friends of the deceased would have reacted if they knew that their dearly departed was lying unattended in the Ho Chunk Casino's parking lot while the driver was inside, placing his bets.

I got lucky as soon as I sat down at a slot machine at the Greektown Casino—a butterfly machine. I like machines with brightly lit symbols like butterflies, chili peppers, and wild cherries. I fed the butterflies a twenty-dollar bill; they gave me back $240. I would be smart, I told myself, and when this money was gone, I would leave, since there really wasn't anything to see here other than the slightly different behavior of these players. Like the man at a machine next to me, neatly dressed in a dark business suit, who kept wiping the Bet Max button with a large white handkerchief while he played. Or the old lady a couple of machines down who wore a white glove on her right hand, which she used to pull the arm of the one-armed bandit. I later found out that it's a slot glove—you can buy them at the casino's gift shop to keep your hand clean.

After I won on the butterfly machine, I began to wonder if Brenda was right, that I was blessed with a special vibe that guided me to winning machines. I knew before I put my money in the machine that the pretty butterflies would bring me luck.

I cashed in my voucher with every intention of leaving. But a Monte Carlo machine caught my attention. I decided that since I was probably one of the few people in the casino who had actually been to Monte Carlo, the machine would bring me more luck. But my efforts to conjure up a win on the Monte Carlo machine were disrupted by a young woman and her grandmother who thought it was okay to stand behind me and run their mouths.

"Look, Granny, see, she's playing three credits."

"Oh, she just got a hit! See how the three dollar signs lit up and lined up on the payline?"

"That's a good one."

"Oh, but this is only a quarter machine. If it had been a dollar machine, she would've won a lot of money."

I felt like turning around and yelling, "Why don't you and your granny go somewhere else? I'm not here to demonstrate how this machine works."

Something was happening to me. I was getting downright mean. I lost all the money I'd won on the butterfly machine and blamed it on the woman and her granny. The busybodies broke my concentration, disrupted the vibe I had going with the Monte Carlo machine. I left Greektown feeling the same sickness that had taken hold of me at the Blue Chip in Indiana. "It's these spaces," I told myself. "They're making me sick."

♦♦♦

Before heading out on the expressway to Orchard Lake, I drove around downtown. The place is depressing. So far none of the casinos, all within two miles of each other, or the much-touted elevated people mover have done anything to bring the city's moribund center back to life. Nor does the annual Detroit International Auto Show bring in enough money to make a difference in downtown Detroit. Celebrities, millionaires, and journalists from around the world come to Detroit for the auto show, stay a few days, spend a lot of money in a few places, and leave. Afterward the city settles back down, much of it unaffected by the occasional big events held downtown, like the 2006 Super Bowl. Restaurants and bars that opened downtown specifically to accommodate the thousands of people who came to see the Pittsburgh Steelers beat the Seattle Seahawks closed shortly after it was over, leaving the city as desolate as it was before.

The city's center is a perfect example of what the economist Earl L. Grinols argues is the cannibalizing effect of casino expansion. The three Detroit casinos have barely made a dint in the city's unemployment rate. They pay the state and the City of Detroit millions of dollars in wagering taxes. Yet they have not brought economic development to Michigan, at least not economic development as defined by Grinols: "The increase in the well-being of households from given resources; the creation of greater value by society from its available resources."

A 2006 report from the U.S. Bureau of Labor Statistics ranked Michigan as having the second-highest unemployment rate—7.1 percent—after Mississippi (7.2 percent). The national unemployment rate was 4.4 percent; Detroit's was 7.0 percent. By August of 2009, that figure had jumped to 17.1 percent for the Detroit metropolitan area; the state's unemployment rate was 15.2, the highest in the nation.

One of the problems is that gamblers who are lucky enough to win some money and don't then gamble it away, take it and leave. They don't spend their money locally, mainly because there's nowhere to spend it—no stores worth shopping in unless you like visiting wig shops and dollar stores. It's even hard to find a grocery store in the areas around the casinos.

Two casinos, MGM Grand and MotorCity, are in impoverished areas, yet they have consistently earned higher revenues than Greektown Casino, which is downtown. The area around the MotorCity, which occupies the former Wonder Bread factory, looks like a wasteland, with weed-infested fields, boarded-up houses, and abandoned buildings everywhere. Each casino is conveniently located near expressways so out-of-town gamblers—the tourists—can take their money and run and never see the blight the millions of dollars they leave behind have yet to eradicate.

As I completed my first tour of downtown Detroit in years, I drove around Grand Circus Park to Washington Boulevard. The boulevard lost its grandeur decades ago. I passed what was left of the Sheraton Cadillac Hotel where in the 1960s I worked as a maid, busgirl, and, finally, a waitress in the once plush Motor Bar. (The building was renovated and reopened in 2008 as the Book Cadillac luxury hotel and condominiums.) An uneducated black girl couldn't do much else in those days. Even those who completed high school or college had difficulty finding work in Detroit, especially downtown.

Detroit in the 1960s was as racist as the South. It just didn't hang out the "Whites Only" signs. Instead, merchants and restaurant owners, especially in the downtown areas, prominently displayed signs that read, "WE RESERVE THE RIGHT TO REFUSE SERVICE TO ANYONE." The downtown merchants who did accept our dollars refused to put more than one or two of us behind their lunch or sales counters or at the receptionist desks in their offices. Those of us who managed to slip through the racial barrier learned to live with the racist behavior of our employers and coworkers simply because we needed to earn a living.

That's why I felt a surge of resentment when, in the last chapter of *Nickel and Dimed,* Barbara Ehrenreich questions why, given the low wages and conditions under which they worked, the people she met while undercover didn't demand higher wages or seek out better-paying jobs. She writes, "I was baffled, initially, by what seemed like a certain lack of get-up-and-go on the part of my fellow workers. Why didn't they just leave for a better-paying job, as I did when I moved from the Hearthside to Jerry's?" (two restaurants in Florida where she worked while posing as a poor person).

Ehrenreich seemed to forget that she could escape this life when-ever she wanted and often took "occasional breaks from this life, going home now and then, catching up on e-mail and for conjugal visits." She was a tourist. The people with whom Ehrenreich worked were as stuck and helpless as I was when I worked at the Sheraton Cadillac for reasons that had as much to do with reliable transportation or proximity to child care centers as low wages. In those days public transportation was the only way for most people to get around. Few people in my neighborhood had cars. We took the bus. And there were no child care centers in the 1960s, at least none I knew of that would take little black babies. I couldn't have afforded them anyway, not with what I was earning.

Back then I didn't know how to negotiate for higher wages. I didn't even know that, as an employee, I had certain rights. And nobody was around to ensure that those rights weren't violated. To complain about poor wages or bad treatment—and I received enough bad treatment at the Sheraton Cadillac Hotel, especially from my white *female* supervisors, to fill a book—was to risk losing my job. I was eighteen when I started working there as a maid in 1964. All I knew was that I needed the job. I was in no position to try to change the system or move to a better-paying job. There weren't any for me. So I tried to be the best damn maid on the team.

Completing my tour, I drove to Woodward Avenue. The J. L. Hudson and Kern's department stores, the Grinnell Brothers House of Music, the Woolworth five and dime where I worked behind the ice cream counter for a short time when I was sixteen (I was fired when I could no longer hide the fact that I was pregnant with my second child), Cunningham's Drug Store, Sander's Ice Cream Shop, the Fanny Farmer Candy Shop, and all the other stores and restaurants that once made the avenue a vibrant retail district were shuttered or demolished long ago, casualties of the mall and the mass movement of the city's white residents to the suburbs that began in the early 1950s and accelerated with deliberate speed after Detroit set itself ablaze during the summer of 1967.

◆ ◆ ◆

I remember the day it happened, July 23, 1967. My new boyfriend had taken my children and me to Waterworks Park, just east of the bridge leading to Belle Isle, which lies in the middle of the Detroit River.

Belle Isle was where we usually went during the summer to escape the often unbearable heat of the apartments and flats we lived in at Holcomb and Forest, on the East Side, deep in Detroit's inner city. Belle Isle is the poor people's park. Back then it was always open to the public. You could go there and stay all day, the breezes from the river making even the hottest days and nights pleasurable.

When we tried to go to Belle Isle that day, the bridge was barricaded; we didn't know why. Several policemen were redirecting traffic. They told us Belle Isle was closed. They weren't letting anyone onto the island, so we settled instead for the next best thing, Waterworks Park with its river breezes and shady willow trees.

We hadn't been at the park long, not more than fifteen minutes or so, when we noticed a couple of cops going around talking to people, who would then pack up their blankets and coolers and leave. This was strange for such a hot and muggy Sunday morning. Where was everybody going?

As we watched and wondered, a cop approached and informed us that we had to leave. Something had happened. He said he didn't know what, but they were closing all the public parks and asking everyone to leave. So we did, reluctantly, and headed home, the voices of Martha Reeves and the Vandellas blasting "Heat Wave" from the car's radio as we wondered how else we might beat the heat. By the time we arrived at Holcomb and Forest, word had spread among the people clustered around their apartment steps and the street's few shade trees that a riot had broken out on Twelfth Street.

Twelfth Street was the place to be on weekends when the black-and-tan clubs—featuring black entertainers but frequented by both black and white club goers—closed. Twelfth Street was where the action was. Where the barbecue and pig foot restaurants, the after-hours joints (or blind pigs, as they often were called), and the red light houses didn't even begin to rock until well after midnight. That's when the sportin' life people came out struttin' their stuff, looking for a good game of poker or craps; when the women and men who had finished their forty hours (plus overtime) at one of the big three factories came looking for excitement and some late night soul food; when the cops came looking for blind pigs to bust.

They thought they found one at 9125 Twelfth Street, where the United Civic League for Community Action had its headquarters on the second floor. By 3:30 a.m. the place was packed with league members and their friends dancing to the music of Motown. Joseph Brown, a black undercover cop, was there too, presumably to confirm what the white cops outside believed: that the people inside the club were engaging in illegal activities—gambling, prostitution, selling drugs. The plan was that if Brown didn't come out within ten minutes, the cops waiting outside could assume he'd made a score—the evidence they needed to raid the place.

The cops waited until around 4 a.m., then stormed the club, beating the door in with a sledgehammer and rounding up the revelers. A paddy wagon was brought in. To the surprise and anger of a crowd that had begun gathering in front of the building, the cops started hauling off club members and their guests—more than seventy people.

Someone in the increasingly angry and boisterous crowd threw a bottle. It shattered the back window of a police car that was transporting prisoners to jail. As if that belligerent act were a signal, the crowd spontaneously began breaking store windows. After Newark, New Jersey, had gone up in flames, local community leaders and city officials in Detroit had insisted for a week, in newspaper articles and editorials, that it couldn't happen here—not in their city. But it did. By 8 a.m. on Sunday, July 23, 1967, a riot had broken out in Detroit.

Of course, we didn't know all this while sitting outside on our porches and front steps at Holcomb and Forest. The media hadn't begun to report what had happened the night before. But one of the young men who regularly held court in front of the corner liquor store said he heard that earlier that morning the cops had gone up to Twelfth Street and shot up a bunch of people during a raid at an after-hours joint.

As more rumors and reports of rioting and police brutality buzzed along the Holcomb and Forest grapevine, we could feel the anger and resentment rising along with the heat, which was almost intolerable by now. People turned up the volumes on their transistor radios, releasing an intermittent cacophony of warnings to stay away from the area while the Young Rascals sang about "grooving on a Sunday afternoon" and Martha and the Vandellas invited us to go dancing in the street. All day long we sat outside our hot apartments and waited for something to happen.

And it did. Either that night or the next, I don't recall, someone smashed the front window of the corner liquor store. Young men moved from one business to the next, breaking windows and encouraging bystanders to "come on and get some of this shit!" Men who wouldn't move even a small piece of furniture in their houses, claiming their backs hurt, were seen carrying out cases of booze and whatever else they could get their hands on. Women who I knew would never steal joined in the looting, as did their children.

It was surreal. These people weren't visibly angry. They were simply seizing an opportunity to rebel against long-standing conditions of racism, poverty, and police brutality. A party mood prevailed as they darted in and out of the liquor store, the little grocery store on the adjacent corner of Holcomb and Forest, and the nearby butcher shop, happy to help themselves to a little piece of the American pie.

Then someone set the liquor store on fire. My neighbor Gloria and I worried as we watched the flames. We were both single mothers. She had four children, I had three. The apartments we lived in weren't much—small, dark, smelly, and roach-infested dwellings. But we had done our best to make them pleasant. Our buildings were old and dilapidated: wood frame two-story buildings crammed together in a tight row. Originally intended as two-family flats, they had been divided into six tiny two-, three-, and four-room apartments. My little drab and airless second-floor, four-room apartment was in the rear of the building. I had only one way in and out—down a rickety wooden staircase. If any of the flames roaring on that corner reached just one of the buildings, they all would've gone up. We would've been homeless.

In the 1960s Detroit landlords discriminated at will and had the law on their side in the form of restricted covenants and the pervasive practice of redlining by realtors, bankers, mortgage lenders, and insurance companies. If I'd had money for a nicer place to rent, I could do so only in areas of the city that had been designated red zones—inner-city neighborhoods already densely populated with unemployed and low-wage-earning black people. Even in those neighborhoods, property owners, most of whom were white, refused to rent to black women with children.

If our buildings were destroyed, where would we go? Gloria's parents lived in the same building, in the apartment right behind hers, so she had nothing to fall back on. My parents lived on the northwest side of town, near West Eight Mile Road. There was no way to get to their house without traveling through areas of the city most affected by the looting, rioting, and burning. By Monday morning most public transportation had been suspended and things had gotten so bad that nobody in their right mind would try to drive to rescue me from my home deep in the inner city of Detroit. So my children and I spent the next few days sitting outside on Gloria's front porch, watching as the corner burned down and as the National Guard, ordered into the city by Governor George Romney, began arriving. Nearly seven thousand inexperienced, ill-equipped, and trigger-happy white boys and men were turned loose on Detroit and surrounding areas for two days with devastating results.

We watched as some of the forty-seven hundred federal troops—paratroopers—whom President Lyndon Johnson ordered into

Detroit on July 25, rode up and down our street in trucks, their rifles pointed out, a loud voice warning us not to violate the curfew that was in effect from 9 p.m. to 5:30 a.m. "We have orders to shoot anything that moves, so stay in your houses," the voice bellowed from a megaphone as the trucks drove past our houses late in the evenings, turning the darkened street into an occupied territory.

We were trapped on our block. After the stores were destroyed, we began running low on food. Nobody had any money or transportation, so we sat on Gloria's front porch, shared what little we had between the two families; prayed for an end to the heat wave, the looting, arson, and murder; and hoped that, when it was all over, we would still have a place to live.

When it finally ended, forty-three people had been killed. More than thirteen hundred buildings had been destroyed. Five thousand people had lost their homes. Many more lost their jobs. I was among the lucky ones. I still had a place to live and I still had a job, although my wages were docked for the days I couldn't report to work.

That riot devastated the City of Detroit in ways that even the bloody Race Riots of the summer of 1943 did not. Thirty-four people died then, twenty-five blacks and nine whites. Property damage was estimated at more than $2 million. But the city recovered. After the 1967 riots, it never did.

After a few days in Detroit visiting places that I had tried for many years to forget—including places where I had hid out as a troubled and pregnant teen—I returned to Madison deeply saddened about the condition of the city of my birth. Part of me wishes that I could return and call it home again, but it is in Madison, Wisconsin, that I belong. Fall classes would start soon. I needed to get ready for the new semester. I also needed to prepare for a play I'd been cast in—as the Queen of Hearts in New American Theater's 2005 holiday production of *Alice in Wonderland*.

CHAPTER 8

Queen of Hearts

One day in October of 2005, during one of my many attempts to stay away from casinos, I was going through my e-mail and found an invitation from Northwest Airlines inviting me and its other frequent fliers to take advantage of a new holiday promotion: "Now through December 23, 2005, visit the enhanced WorldPerks Mileage Partners pages on nwa.com, and discover more than 180 easy ways to earn miles. Plus you could instantly win one of over 200 daily prizes from brands like WorldPerks Visa, Lands' End, Hyatt Hotels and Resorts, Bose, and more! Once registered, you're automatically entered into the Grand Prize drawing for a seven-night cruise on Norwegian Cruise Line."

Usually I ignored such e-mails. This time I decided to see if my luck would change in what I considered the safe sphere of my laptop. After all, the invitation ended with "Play Now and Good Luck!," the same encouragement I got from the cheerful and smiling gate keepers at the Grand Victoria Riverboat Casino in Elgin, Illinois.

I followed the instructions, entered my name and World Perks number, and was sent to a webpage that behaved like the "Double Diamond Haywire" machines I'd been trying to make pay me some money during recent visits to Ho Chunk. I guided my cursor to the button that activated all the prizes I could win and watched as their symbols were shuffled and reshuffled. When they finally stopped, none matched the winning picture. I was invited to try again the next day. "Well," I thought, "So much for that."

What would I do if I won a cruise, anyway? I feel about cruises the same as I feel about a trip to Las Vegas. I don't want to be in an environment that encourages excessiveness and overindulgence, especially in the middle of an ocean, because I can't leave when I want to. But that brush with what amounts to a mild and legitimate form of Internet gambling was enough to send me on yet another gambling binge. That and the sudden realization that, as the Queen of Hearts and the Red Queen in New American Theater's holiday production of *Alice in Wonderland*, I was a walking, talking symbol of Casinoland.

◆◆◆

New American Theater was in Rockford, Illinois, halfway between Madison and Chicago, and about thirty-five miles west of the Grand Victoria Riverboat Casino. (The theater closed in 2007). I started auditioning at the theater in June of 2000, but never received even a callback. That wasn't surprising because, frankly, I began auditioning there and at other regional theater companies long before I knew what the hell I was doing.

In those days I thought a monologue was something to be shouted to the back of the room. I knew nothing about motivation, objectives, and creating imaginary people and spaces in an otherwise empty room as I faced the person behind the table, bellowed my monologues, and graciously thanked the poor victim of my efforts to turn myself into an actor. It took more than five years of intensive training and practice in community theater to get good enough that artistic directors of small professional theater companies might be interested in casting me in a show.

By the time I stood before New American Theater's new artistic director during the annual June general auditions, I felt confident that I'd acquired the skills I needed to work in his theater. I walked into the rehearsal space, introduced myself, performed my two monologues, and then felt the weight of silence descend on me. The director didn't say anything. I'm not sure he even looked at me. He was reading the résumé I'd attached to the back of my headshot. I thanked him for hearing me and started to leave. But the silence was too much. I said, "Do you have any questions or anything you want to ask me?" I don't remember what he said. I just remember his silence and thinking that I needed to keep a positive attitude and remember that auditioning and getting rejected is about 99 percent of an actor's job.

I drove back to Madison feeling a bit defeated but determined not to let the director's unresponsiveness get the best of me. I was therefore truly surprised when he called me in late September to ask if I was going to be busy for the next two months. Of course, I wasn't busy! It's amazing how quickly actors can clear their calendars when someone wants to cast us in a show. He wanted to cast me in *Alice in Wonderland* as the Queen of Hearts, the Red Queen, Alice's mother, and a Daisy voice. I happily accepted the roles.

We began rehearsals on October 18, 2005, four days after the death of my oldest brother. He was the first of my six siblings to depart this world. His death came as a shock to us all. He lived in California and didn't stay much in touch with the rest of us. We found out that he had been hospitalized and was being treated for lymphoma just two days before he died unexpectedly of septic shock. We were devastated. Why didn't anyone let us know that our brother was seriously ill? The rehearsals gave me relief from my anguish. After all, *Alice in Wonderland* has nothing to do with reality, and the director had assembled a great group of actors and designers.

We set to work in earnest to create a holiday fantasy delight and had fun doing it, despite the long hours and the tediousness of repetition, especially during "tech" week when light and sound cues and costumes are added. I attended my brother's funeral in Los Angeles and returned to a heavy rehearsal schedule, three stacks of papers to grade, and lectures to prepare for my classes at the university. Not to mention the three hours a day I was now spending traveling to and from Rockford. My busy schedule kept me out of the casinos for a few weeks.

We opened *Alice in Wonderland* on Tuesday, November 15, 2005. The next day I embarked on yet another gambling binge. I decided that since Rockford is close to Chicago, I should try to see some plays on the days we didn't have late shows and I didn't have to rush back to Madison. I wanted to see *Bright Abyss* at Chicago Shakespeare Theater at Navy Pier. This was part of the theater's international guest artist program. The French troupe that was visiting is famous for its avant-garde, physical theater. I withdrew $200 from my checking account, ordered my $48 ticket online, reserved a room at La Quinta Inn in Hoffman Estates (on I-90, an hour east of Rockford and forty-five minutes southwest of Chicago) for $64, including taxes, and set out for the Windy City right after our evening performance.

By the time I got to Elgin—only eight miles shy of Hoffman Estates—I had decided to stop by the Grand Victoria Casino and try to win some money. My plan was to win $200 and deposit it into my checking account. I sailed past the smiling gatekeepers who wished me luck and quickly won $250 by betting $20 on a five-dollar Wild Cherry machine. Common sense should've made me stop. I'd reached my goal within about fifteen minutes. But gamblers don't use common sense.

Back then I thought that what keeps gamblers gambling is greed. I wasn't yet convinced that the highly stimulating environment created by slot machines in casinos was causing people to become addicted. It would take a few more years, many losses, and lots of therapy for me to come to that conclusion.

I left the Grand Victoria after about forty-five minutes with $30 less than I'd arrived with. I'd lost $280 trying to win jackpots on some of the two-dollar machines. I was so agitated by the time I got to the theater that I could hardly enjoy the show. I returned to my hotel and slept soundly. I was exhausted.

The next day I headed back to Madison after our morning children's show, but in Rockford an enormous billboard for Ho Chunk Casino that loomed over Highway 2 was too much to resist. I drove right past Madison to Ho Chunk. I was there from about 4 p.m. until 9 p.m., hating myself every moment. By 8 p.m. I had taken $100—all I would allow myself—and raised it to $500 and then lost almost all of it again. Then I hit a jackpot—$1,900 on a five-times pay machine. I asked for a check, which I tucked safely away in my pants pocket. But instead of leaving, I kept on playing. I had about $84 left on my cash voucher. I went to the Wild Cherry machine and got lucky again.

Before I realized what was happening, I'd won $700 and lost it all! Part of me kept saying that I had all the money I needed in my pocket. The check was safe. If I had left, I would've had $2,600 to put into my checking account to help pay for the new Lennox furnace and air conditioner I needed—or rather, the new comfort system that promised to deliver high indoor air quality—that I had scheduled for installation a few weeks hence. Instead, I convinced myself that I could lose this money since I had not earned it. I finally left, disgusted with myself. I kept asking myself, why would an otherwise normal person deliberately gamble away $700?

The next night I was back at the Grand Victoria Casino trying to get the $700 back. I arrived late, around 11:30 p.m. The place was packed. I realized that I'd been in a casino this late at night only once before, at Potawatomi, where all kinds of gambling was going on. Ho Chunk didn't have roulette, dice, and poker then. The only table game was blackjack, so Ho Chunk was quiet by comparison. I was amazed by the noise, energy, and diversity of the "guests," some of whom were walking around with big wads of money in their hands.

People were laughing and shouting at the table games; others were playing two and three slot machines at a time. I passed by a woman who had just hit a jackpot on a $25 machine. I couldn't tell what the machine paid out, but I noticed she had $825 worth of credits. I was curious, but I wasn't about to ask her what she had won. I always resented people flocking to my winning machine to congratulate and touch me. It's bad manners.

Another woman was frantically banging on the Bet Max button on her machine. Occasionally, she would pull the lever and then grab the machine with both hands, as if she were trying to shake money out of it. The machine didn't move. It didn't give her any money, either. She was agitated and smoking furiously.

Everywhere I looked, people were smoking like trains. Now, I was about to spend $6,100 on a "comfort system" to keep me cozy and improve the air quality in my house, and I always insisted on a smoke-free room whenever I checked into a hotel, but here I was exposing myself to second-hand smoke every time I stepped into a casino. Gamblers smoke like fiends and don't care if they're blowing smoke in your face. They're not polite.

I lost $200 within about forty-five minutes. I went to my hotel and took a long hot shower. I felt dirty, like I was covered with grime. The next day, after the morning performance of *Alice in Wonderland*, I drove back to Ho Chunk Casino with $300, still determined to win back my money. I was there only about an hour when I doubled that amount on a "double pay" machine. I won $300 more on a Wild Cherry machine. I now had a voucher worth $900. Then I repeated what I'd done just two days earlier. I went to the progressive jackpot machines and quickly lost all the money.

This time I felt relieved. I decided I really didn't want that money. I left thinking that the way to acquire extra income was not by roaming around casinos like a crazy person or some kind of automaton, sticking $100 bills into slot machines, and hoping for increasingly bigger payouts. My nerves were on edge, not only because of the noise and smoke and the stress of winning and losing what for me was lots of money, but because I knew I'd stepped way over the line. I was on the verge of becoming a compulsive gambler.

As I drove home that night, I kept saying to myself, you cannot continue doing this. It will kill you.

◆ ◆ ◆

That night I had a terrible dream. This time I was in Wonderland. But it wasn't Alice's Wonderland. It was the wonderland of casinos— Casinoland. Some of the crazier characters with whom I'd spent the last few weeks were there: the Rabbit, the Mad Hatter, the March Hare, the Cheshire Cat, the Dutchess, and lots of card soldiers. They were all playing poker and laughing like crazy. Only they weren't wearing the familiar friendly faces of my fellow actors. They looked more like the sketches in Lewis Carroll's book—mean and menacing. The Cheshire Cat's disembodied head kept following me around as I tried to find the right machine in the "Hall of Slot Machines," the one that would let me out of this increasingly long, narrow, and crowded space.

"Which way out?" I asked the Cat.

"Go that way," he replied, tilting his head to the left. "And try this machine."

His head floated over to a Wild Cherry machine and hovered there.

I tried to put a hundred-dollar bill in the slot. The machine kept spitting it out.

"This machine won't take my money," I cried in despair.

"Then try another one." The Cat's smile was looking more and more wicked.

I tried stuffing the hundred-dollar bill in one machine after another, looking for the one that would let me out of the Hall of Slot Machines. The machines kept spitting it out. I was growing more and more frustrated. I was tired of the noise and the crazy laughing of the Wonderland characters, who had begun to taunt me as I tried to find my way out.

"You stupid bitch," hollered the March Hare. "I saw you. I saw how many cherries lit up. That Wild Cherry machine paid you a lotta money. But you weren't satisfied. You got greedy, didn't you? You should've taken your

money and left when you had a chance. Now you can't get out. You're stuck here with us, don't you know? Why don't you go and get one of those player club cards and tether yourself to the machines like all these other fools walking around here? You might as well earn some points while you're losing your life. You can trade them in for some of the junk they offer. Or maybe a meal. Buy some more hotdogs, since you like them so much."

The Mad Hatter just stood there giggling and drinking his endless cup of tea, while the Cheshire Cat's head floated above one Wild Cherry machine after another, teasing me with the hope that this one will be the way out.

"Please, Cheshire Puss, these machines won't take my money. How am I ever going to get out of here?"

"Who said you were going to get out at all?" he snarled. "You have to stay here with us. This is where mad people belong. That's why we're here, you see. We're all mad. And so are you. You must be. Why else would you come here? You must be mad." The Cheshire Cat's head was getting larger as he kept repeating, "You must be mad. Why else would you come here? You must be mad. We're all mad here, you see. You must be mad!"

◆ ◆ ◆

I managed to get through the rest of the long run of *Alice in Wonderland*—it closed on December 30, 2005—without experiencing another casino attack, mainly because of the tremendous energy I was expending both onstage and off, traveling back and forth to Rockford four days a week, teaching my classes at the university, and attending meetings of the various committees I served on. I also got a sudden wake-up call. I had gone to dinner at a friend's house and picked up the November, 2005 issue of *Chicago* magazine. It featured an article titled "Betting Her Life," which chronicled the near-fatal gambling experiences of Barbara Hermansen, a successful Illinois attorney.

I took the magazine home and sat up late that night reading the article. It hit too close to home for my comfort. It described how Hermansen nearly lost everything: her family, her home, and her life after visiting Las Vegas during the summer of 2001 and becoming addicted to playing slot machines. Within weeks of her trip to Las Vegas, Hermansen was gambling online and at the Grand Victoria Riverboat Casino, losing thousands of dollars.

According to the article, when Hermansen first visited the Grand Victoria, "She was immediately hooked. This was gambling. Machines whirring, cards flying. Smoky, yes, but she couldn't have cared less. All she could see was rows and rows of shining slot machines, the only game she played. So many possibilities. If one machine was cold, she would simply move to another. She would start betting small, then gradually increase her wagers. Before she knew it, she would be utterly engrossed, exactly like the poor mesmerized souls she had pitied years ago" [when she and her husband visited a riverboat casino in Indiana].

Reading about Barbara Hermansen was like reading about myself, like someone had written my story. Like Hermansen, I had no interest in casinos before my first visit to Ho Chunk in April of 2005. A visit to the casino in Monte Carlo in June of 1991—the first time I'd ever been inside one—was followed by commercial bookings at Potawatomi Casino in Milwaukee in December of 2000 and Jack Binion's Horseshoe Casino in Hammond, Indiana, and a trip to MotorCity Casino in Detroit with my sisters during a Thanksgiving trip home in 2004. That had been plenty for me. It was depressing.

Although casino ads invariably feature well-dressed and happy people enjoying winning lots of money at craps and blackjack tables and slot machines, most habitual casino patrons are indeed "poor mesmerized souls." I remember being astonished to see so many people sitting in front of slot machines when I once arrived at Potawatomi Casino at 5 a.m. for a photo shoot. I wondered if they had been there all night.

There were maybe five or six models there for that morning's shoot. After we got dressed and our hair and makeup were done, we were led to a blackjack table. I sat down and reached for one of the stacks of chips arranged on the table and was quickly and sternly reprimanded by a man in a dark brown suit—a pit boss, I suppose—

who was standing near the table, a security guard by his side. "Ma'am, don't touch the chips! Keep your hands off the table!" I put my hands in my lap and mumbled something about the chips being nothing but worthless pieces of plastic. The dealer laughed and said, "I see you know nothing about blackjack!" I didn't. I still don't.

As a commercial print model, I work with props most of the time. I didn't know that this was the real deal. The woman dealing the cards was a real blackjack dealer. Those plastic chips represented real money, at least in the casino. Everything at that table was for real. Except the models. We were the props. The fakes. The pretenders. We had been hired to help promote casino gambling as entertainment, a leisure activity, but I didn't see anyone there that morning who looked as if they were being entertained. They looked tired, uptight, and frustrated. That I would become one of them never crossed my mind.

◆◆◆

Slot machine gambling is a solitary activity. The deeper slot players can disappear into the recesses of the casino, the better. They're unsociable. They don't want to be bothered when they're trying to grind money out of the machines. Most slot players are not high rollers. They come with very small bankrolls, hoping to win some money while they're zoning out. They smoke like chimneys. They bang on the machines. Some of them pray; others curse. I've even see slot players wave their hands like magic wands, back and forth over the monitor, or touch the top of the machine as if they were trying to bless it or conjure up a muse or some other spirit with the power to bring them the hoped for jackpot. And they complain bitterly about how the casino does nothing but rip them off.

One day I sat next to a woman who said she had been at her machine, a twelve-times-pay machine, all afternoon and still hadn't won any money. After hitting the Bet Max button with her fist a few times to prove it wasn't doing anything—she kept saying, "See, what did I tell you?"—she called an attendant. She complained to him that the machine must be broken since all it was doing was taking her money. The attendant looked at her and said, "Ma'am, that's what gambling's about. There's nothing wrong with that machine." He was shaking his head as he walked away.

Another time, a man near me called an attendant to complain that his machine would *not* take his money. He had been trying to stuff a wrinkled hundred-dollar bill in the "Wheel of Fortune" machines and they kept rejecting it. Frustrated, he called an attendant. "These machines won't take my money." The attendant called over a money changer, who exchanged the bill for a crisp new one. "I guarantee you they will take your money," the attendant added as he walked away.

Some of the players at the "Wheel of Fortune" machines apparently found the attendant's remark funny. They laughed. I thought it was all a bit absurd. To complain about machines taking our money and then complain when they don't! I took advantage of this momentary levity to ask a question: "Is anybody having fun?" More nervous laughter and a unanimous and resounding no! I looked around. They hadn't even bothered to take their eyes off their machines to see who had spoken to them. They just kept right on spinning, mesmerized by the sounds, symbols, and blinking lights of the slot machines and the labyrinthine layout of the casino floor.

What I found particularly troubling about Barbara Hermansen's story is how quickly she reached a point of no return. The labyrinth wasn't just the physical space of the casino; it was also in her head—a compulsion that took precedence over everything else—her children, her husband, her home. Whenever she wasn't gambling, she was thinking, planning her next visit to the Grand Victoria Riverboat and making up excuses, or rather lies, about where she was going or had been. Her compulsion got so bad that she had herself barred from Illinois casinos. It didn't stop her from gambling. She simply drove to the riverboat casinos in Indiana and continued to lose thousands of dollars.

After trying everything, including seeing a psychiatrist, Hermansen decided to commit suicide. She would go to the Elder Lane Beach, where she often swam alone, and drown herself but make it look like an accident. It was a carefully laid-out plan. She would make it look as if she had been collecting sea glass, decided to take a swim, then couldn't make it back to the shore.

Only she couldn't carry it out. She called a friend who took her to the Evanston Northwestern Hospital where she was given a sedative and put under suicide watch. However, even after spending nine days in the psychiatric ward, working with a therapist specializing in compulsive disorders, and seeing her marriage nearly destroyed, Hermansen couldn't stay away from slot machines. She kept on gambling until a therapist suggested that there might be a link between her gambling behavior and a medication she was taking to ease her restless leg syndrome. She stopped taking the medication and her compulsive gambling ceased.

Hermansen's story frightened me. This was my first time reading about someone who didn't fit the stereotype of gambler, that is, someone who usually is male and a high or low roller lurking around in casinos in Las Vegas or Atlantic City. Although white and from a much more privileged background, Barbara Hermansen was too much like me for my comfort: a woman caught up in something she was not prepared to deal with and didn't understand. Her story raised many questions, like why I continued to be drawn to a place that offered me no enjoyment and was sucking my soul right out of me.

What's there to enjoy anyway in a place where daylight and time are deliberately blotted out? The overwhelming smell of cigarette and cigar smoke, the relentless sounds of the slot machines, the blinking lights and electronic displays, and the labyrinthine layout of the casinos I visited had the quality of a nightmare, but I kept right on going.

With each visit the casino was becoming more like a colorfully lit hell. There was a sense of unreality about the space and my presence in it. Each time I entered a casino, I felt I was leaving behind all that was familiar to me, everything that kept me safe and comfortable, and descending into a cavernous and hellish place where great harm awaited. I felt like I was playing with my own destruction, punishing myself for something I had done but couldn't name. Even when I won money—especially when I won money—I felt nervous, anxious. But why?

After reading about Barbara Hermansen, my obsession with writing a book about gambling intensified. Rather than confront the real problem, my increasing addiction to slot machines, I decided to turn myself into a researcher and study the "phenomenon" of casino gambling. It was the only way I knew to save myself. Books have always been my lifeline. At that point I need one badly. Little did I know that it would take more than a book to keep me safe and sane.

CHAPTER 9

Slot Machine Sickness

For most of 2006 I spent my spare time reading dense academic articles and books on casino gambling and writing the first draft of what would become this book. I also wrote scathing and unpublishable attacks on gambling industry insiders like Marten Jensen, Victor H. Royer, and MacIntyre Symms, whose books on how to beat the slots are so full of nonsense and so-called strategies for winning that they should have kept me away from the casinos. I continued to go, but less frequently. Barbara Hermansen's story had affected me deeply. I kept the title page of her article on my desk. Her image on that page haunted me. I saw myself going down her path, especially at the Grand Victoria Riverboat Casino where I'd begun to play $25 slots, thereby intensifying my stress. My behavior was troubling, frightful even, for all the reasons Hermansen mentioned in her article. And there seemed to be no explanation for it. Unlike Hermansen, I couldn't attribute my gambling to medication. I wasn't taking any.

The 2002 *New York Times* article that first suggested such a link to Hermansen also cites other kinds of compulsive, rewards-based behaviors that put our brains on "automatic pilot," that is, "they operate outside of conscious awareness." An example is when we carry out routine activities such as driving to work along the same route or hitting the brakes when we come to a red light. Our brain automatically activates the circuits governing decision making. However, when it comes to rewards, if we get more than we expect, our brain vigorously fires dopamine neurons; if we get less, the dopamine system quiets down. This fluctuation is what makes people crave things.

According to Dr. Gregory Berns, a psychiatrist at the Emory University School of Medicine in Atlanta, "Winning in gambling can . . . hijack the dopamine system. . . . Many people visit a casino, lose money and are not tempted to go back. But compulsive gamblers seem to have vulnerable dopamine systems. . . . The first time they win, they get a huge dopamine rush that gets embedded in their memory. They keep gambling and the occasional dopamine rush of winning overrides their conscious knowledge that they will lose in the long run." Every gambler will lose in the *long run*, as I did before my behavior and Barbara Hermansen's story scared me into making a greater effort to stop. What troubled me about Hermansen is that she *lost* her first time in the casino. She lost most of the time, except for a $68,000 jackpot she won at the Horseshoe Casino in Hammond, Indiana. By the time she hit that jackpot the family was in serious financial trouble.

The studies cited in the *New York Times* article strongly suggest that people taking medication that affects the dopamine system, which is what Hermansen was taking, are vulnerable to compulsive gambling. What the article didn't explain is why other people, like me, who don't take any medication, also are vulnerable. Does it have to do with my "addictive personality," as my colleague Michael Thornton once suggested to me?

Another thing that troubled me is that some of the essays I read seemed to relieve people of responsibility for our actions. Even Barbara Hermansen questioned whether the "drug could make someone do such unspeakable things—lie to her husband, or get behind the wheel of a car and drive to a casino." I often asked myself similar questions: What's making me get into my car on a beautiful, sunny day when I would rather be working in my garden, or late at night when I could be reading a good book or sleeping, and go to a place that makes me sick, nauseates me, and causes me so much emotional turmoil? I'd say to myself, "You don't have to be here. You made this choice."

I often looked around at the employees at Ho Chunk Casino, women and men who had to be there because they needed their jobs. I *chose* to come and give away more money in a day than they probably earned in a week. For all the exciting work that's going on in neuroscience about our brains and how they function, I worried that such studies will make it too easy for us to excuse our behavior and say, "It's not my fault. Dopamine made me do it."

But why do some people go to casinos, spend a few dollars playing the slots, and then leave while others, like Barbara Hermansen (and me) risk everything, even our lives, for the chance to win the ever elusive jackpot, *knowing* the odds are against us? Is compulsive slot machine gambling an addiction?

Experts are divided, mainly because they can't agree on what constitutes an addiction. Some specialists in substance abuse define addiction as a physiological dependence resulting from the use of chemical substances, a disease. Others define addiction as persistent and harmful behavioral excesses that may not be chemically induced but cause serious physiological and psychological problems. Psychologists use the terms *compulsive* and *pathological* to describe gamblers who can't seem to stop, although they know they're ruining their lives.

I don't know what category I fall in. I've never been big on labels anyway. I just knew that what I was doing was very bad for me. Still, I decided to respond to some of the questions provided by Gamblers Anomynous on its website just to see if I was as bad off as Barbara Hermansen and some of the other people, especially elderly people, whose stories I'd occasionally run across in magazines and on the Internet.

◆ ◆ ◆

Q. Did you ever lose time from work or school due to gambling?

A. Nope. I don't teach during the summer, so I didn't have to worry about losing time at work or school, although I did cancel one of my piano lessons to go to Ho Chunk with Bev. Once school started, I went to the casino only at night or on weekends.

Q. Has gambling ever made your home life unhappy?

A. My home life was unhappy before I went to the casino because I was still trying to get over the ugly breakup with the man I had lived with for many years. Gambling didn't make my unhappy home life any more or less unhappy since I was the only one there.

Q. Did gambling affect your reputation?

A. No, because aside from my family, nobody knew I was gambling. However, I was concerned that my reputation might be ruined if the university people knew I was hanging out at Ho Chunk Casino. I was especially concerned that if I won a really big jackpot, like a million dollars, and got my picture in the paper holding a giant cardboard check, state legislators would read about it and all hell would break loose. I can hear them now: "See, those professors are up at Ho Chunk Casino gambling when they should be in their offices talking to students or at home writing articles and books. Let's vote to cut the university's budget. Let's freeze their salaries!" So as far as my reputation is concerned, it is what it is. That's all I can say.

Q. Have you ever felt remorse after gambling?

A. I always felt remorse, even when I won.

Q. Did you ever gamble to get money with which to pay debts or to otherwise solve financial difficulties?

A. Not really. After winning a couple of jackpots during my first visits to Ho Chunk, I was set financially for the summer, which was my only financial difficulty. Once, in November 2005, I went to Ho Chunk to win some money to help pay for a new furnace, but it wasn't necessary for me to gamble to get the money. By the way, I won $1,900 that night. Well, $1,800, when you deduct the $100 I wagered.

Q. After a win, did you have a strong urge to return and win more?

A. Not right away. After a win I just wanted to get the hell out of the casino and never go back. The urge to return and win more money usually didn't set in for several days. Sometimes several weeks.

Q. Did you often gamble until your last dollar was gone?

A. I've often gambled until the last dollar I brought with me was gone. I'm not stupid enough to gamble away every dollar I have to my name.

Q. Did you ever borrow to finance your gambling?

A. It depends on what you mean by *borrow*. Are you talking about borrowing money on my credit card? From my checking or savings accounts? If you're asking me if I borrowed money from a family member or acquaintance, or borrowed money that didn't belong to me, like in stealing, then, no. But I took out advances on my credit card when I ran out of cash while at the casino. A credit card advance is a loan, isn't it? A loan is something you borrow, right? So maybe the answer is yes, maybe no. It depends on how I'm supposed to interpret what you mean by *borrow*.

Q. Did you ever gamble longer than you planned?

A. No. I never planned to gamble for any specific length of time, just long enough to either win or lose some money. Which doesn't take much time, usually fifteen to forty-five minutes, which is about as long as I can bear to be in a casino.

Q. Did gambling cause you to have difficulty sleeping?

A. Yes, even when I won money.

◆ ◆ ◆

After taking the gambling test I decided I was not really that bad off, certainly not as bad as all those frustrated-looking people roaming around Ho Chunk Casino sticking their money and their rewards cards into the slots. Those people had problems. You could see it in their faces. Nope! I could quit gambling anytime I wanted and not miss it one bit. That's what I kept telling myself, even as I was getting in my car to go to Ho Chunk or to the Grand Victoria Riverboat Casino. Plus, if I were going to write about casino gambling, I needed to continue my research.

I was in so much denial as I struggled through dense academic articles about gambling and economic development, addiction and the effects of slot machines on the chemistry in our brains that I had convinced myself that my trips to the casinos in 2006 were all in the interest of my research. In fact, the work was the excuse I needed to try and try again to win the jackpot I was sure awaited me. It was as if my personality—or maybe my brain—had split in half. One part was rational: it guided me to the National Center for Responsible Gaming's website, where I found a list of articles that have been published in peer-reviewed journals about gambling disorders. The irrational part kept sending me back to the casinos, back to the places that were making me sick.

◆ ◆ ◆

Since 1996, when NCRG was founded, the gambling industry has contributed more than $15 million for research on gambling problems, including the effects of slots playing on people's brains. The research is conducted by an international team of scientists, scholars, and academics, many of whom are connected to the Harvard University Medical School's Institute for Research on Pathological Gambling and Related Disorders. The institute was established in 2000. Like the National Center for Responsible Gaming, the institute is funded by the American Gaming Association and International Gaming Technology, a major manufacturer of slot machines.

After reading articles in the NCRG's bibliography and some fun stuff too, like the neurosurgeon Katrina Firlik's book, *Another Day in the Frontal Lobe,* I decided to try to get my brain imaged. I wanted to know how neuroscientists go about their work. During a visit to my doctor for a routine annual checkup, I asked her if she would order a Functional Magnetic Resonance Imaging (fMRI) test because something was wrong with my brain. She asked a few questions, like whether I was feeling dizzy, having headaches or blurred vision, or was losing consciousness. I told her no. "Then there's nothing wrong with your brain," she said. I didn't tell her the real reason I needed my head examined.

As luck would have it, a few weeks later I received an e-mail invitation to join a study by researchers at the Wisconsin Comprehensive Memory Program about the onset of Alzheimer's Disease. I think every university employee older than fifty got that e-mail. The researchers were looking for people with a family history of Alzheimer's disease, people with mild cognitive impairment, and healthy normal volunteers. I think I fell somewhere between the second and third categories. I'm sure I became cognitively impaired every time I stepped inside a casino. No medication was involved in the research project. If I passed the prescreening, I would do one day of memory tests, and the next day my brain would be scanned while I repeated some of the same tests inside the machine.

The prescreening test was nothing more than a telephone interview by a technician working on the study. I think all the technicians were doctoral students in psychology and neuroscience. One question was whether I had muddled thinking. I told her yes. I'm a professor; my thinking is muddled most of the time. She wanted to know whether I had a problem with alcohol or substance abuse. I told her yes—I'm a great abuser of Kendall Jackson's chardonnay and zinfindel. She asked whether I had any metal in my head or elsewhere in my body. Yes, I have screws in my head, literally—four dental implants on titanium screws.

The technician took the information. She called back a couple of days later and said that although there was concern about the alcohol abuse (throughout this gambling ordeal I'd become increasingly dependent on my favorite brand of chardonnay) and the screws in my head, I'd been accepted into the study and would be paid $50 for the two days (the only money I received from the university or any other institution or organization for this book).

I was a lousy subject. I was more interested in the equipment and the kinds of cognitive tests that were being done—looking at faces on a computer and trying to remember the order in which they appeared, being given a list of words and trying to remember them—than whatever it was the technicians were trying to get me to do. The only reason I joined the study was to see how neuroscientists conduct the kind of research I read about in the articles from the National Center for Responsible Gaming and to get a picture of my brain.

On the second day I was put into the fMRI machine. I wore a pair of goggles that worked like a computer screen. They reflected some of the images I'd seen on a computer the previous day. I was instructed to repeat the tests I had done before, this time by pushing a button on a little remote device they gave me as they scanned my brain. The technicians started the tests. The machine made horrible loud noises, like somebody was standing next to my ear with a jack hammer.

I was in the machine for only about fifteen minutes when the voice of the technician conducting the scan informed me that they were discontinuing it. The screws in my head were distorting the images they were trying to photograph as I performed the cognitive tasks. They wanted to see what parts of my brain lit up when I did certain prescribed things. The technician told me that since I was there, in the fMRI machine, they would go ahead and take pictures of my brain and give them to me as a souvenir.

They printed the pictures out on regular printer paper and gave them to me before I left, black-and-white images of my very healthy brain. I was disappointed. I was expecting color copies. I was going to frame the photos and hang them on the walls in my living room. I thought they would make nice little art works, something interesting to show my friends when they visited—colorful pictures of my brain. I left the Waisman Lab for Brain Imaging and Behavior, where the tests had been conducted, thinking that the experience of sitting in front of a slot machine can't be replicated in a laboratory setting. The sounds, lights, and smells aren't there.

A few weeks later technicians working for one of the world's most prominent neuroscientists, Dr. Richard Davidson, sent out an e-mail looking for subjects to participate in a study on the effects of meditation on the brain. Davidson has spent thirty years studying the brains of meditating monks and wanted to know whether meditation could change the brain chemistry of the rest of us and increase our happiness. In this study all you had to do was go to yoga classes and meditate for about forty-five minutes a day. Perfect, I thought. That's just what I needed to break the hold the slots had on me.

The study was to last eight weeks, the yoga classes were free, and participants would be paid $50. I called right away and said I was interested. There was one problem, though. At the end of the study participants would have their brains scanned. I told the technician about the previous study and about the dental implants. She said that would disqualify me. I was disappointed again. I was sure that the meditation study under the direction of Dr. Richard Davidson and his team of researchers was the cure I needed. By the end of 2006 my gambling had once again spiraled way out of control.

CHAPTER 10

The Gamblers

Daddy, why do you want to celebrate your ninety-first birthday at MotorCity Casino?

Cause that's what I want to do. Due to the fact that I don't know how many years I got left on this earth, I want to do what I want to do how I want to do it. And that's that.

It's New Year's Eve, 2006. I've come to Detroit to bring in the New Year with my father. We had Christmas dinner at my daughter's house in Orchard Lake. Then I took off for Philadelphia to attend the Modern Language Association Conference. The conference is always held December 27–30, which is one of the reasons I stopped going once I received tenure.

Attending the Modern Language Association Conference is a necessary evil of my profession. You have to go to the MLA to interview for a job; you have to go to the MLA to establish your presence in the world of literary scholars once you've got a job. Well, my presence was well established by December of 2006. I have nothing else to prove to anybody about anything. Plus, I've got better things to do during the holidays than sit around hotels and conference centers with a bunch of literature professors and overeager graduate students. I agreed to go this time because our department had been authorized to make two hires, two new assistant professors, and I wanted to be part of the interview team. I also wanted to meet one of Pennsylvania's most outspoken opponents of casino expansion, Bill Kearney.

I came across Kearney while looking for stories about casino gambling that weren't set in Las Vegas. He had written a book titled *Comped*, a fictionalized account of how, in less than two years, he went from being a successful businessman to losing everything—his wife, family, and business—after getting hooked on high-stakes blackjack in Atlantic City casinos. I saw the book on Amazon.com and was shocked by the price: $50 for a paperback that originally sold for $15, so I sent an e-mail to his web address and asked, "What's this book written on? Gold leaf paper?" He promptly e-mailed back and suggested I try another site that sells books about gambling. I didn't find it. Somebody obviously had jacked up the price because that was the only copy available. Anyway, Bill Kearney included in his message a letter he sends to just about anybody who'll listen, expressing his concern about the proliferation of casinos in the state of Pennsylvania. He also sent audio and video links to the radio and television talk shows on which he has appeared to argue against the expansion of casino gambling.

I was interested in what Kearney had to say because I found it bewildering that, aside from the sociologists and economists who study the casino gambling industry, there seemed to be little opposition to what Kearney calls "casino breeding" in the places of most concern to me: Wisconsin, where I live, and Detroit, my hometown. I hadn't heard the voices of people at the grassroots level. Their silence suggested to me that they might be unaware of the industry's potential to destroy the economic infrastructure of local communities, especially communities of color such as Detroit, which can't afford to take any more financial hits. Maybe they had bought the rhetoric of their lawmakers about how casinos are going to bring new jobs and economic recovery to their cities. Or maybe they didn't know what to ask about the economic and social impacts of casino encroachment.

There's a sense of urgency in what Bill Kearney has to say. The Commonwealth of Pennsylvania passed a gaming bill in 2004 that allowed for fourteen slots-only casinos and racinos—slots parlors at race tracks—to operate in the state over the next few years. Kearney wants the casino industry to be more accountable for what it's putting out there, its "product": time spent and money lost at the slot machines.

Before I left Detroit, I sent an e-mail to Kearney informing him that I would be at the Marriott Hotel and Convention Center in Philadelphia and asked if he would meet with me. He agreed. Right after the other professor and I finished interviewing our last candidate, I packed my things and headed to the lobby to wait for him. It wasn't hard to pick him out in the crowd of literature professors. Bill Kearney stands out. A tall, imposing figure dressed in black with beautiful, thick silver hair and piercing blue eyes, he looks like he can take on the mob all by himself. Kearney's on a mission and has become a real thorn in the side of Pennsylvania state legislators and gaming regulators. He just won't shut up or go away. Every chance he gets, he's in the face of the people who control gambling in his state, demanding they show some accountability for what they've unleashed on their citizens.

We went into the hotel's coffee shop. Kearney wasted no time with getting-to-know-you niceties; he was ready to talk. I sat there marveling at this man's energy. One moment he was raging about what was happening to his community; in another moment his gentle side showed as he talked about the dangers to which we're exposing our children and grandchildren as we sit by idly and let the casinos "breed" or expand throughout the country. Kearney knows that casinos and gambling are here to stay. As he explained to me, once they slip into a community, you've lost. You have to fight to keep them out.

Kearney's battle with the casino industry isn't on moral grounds. He lost a fortune gambling, and although he blames nobody but himself, he believes that casinos bear some responsibility for the growing numbers of people who are betting themselves into financial ruin. Since our meeting Kearney has kept me abreast of his efforts to get the gaming law amended to keep check cashing services and ATMs out of casinos, ban free booze (Pennsylvania casinos can serve complimentary alcoholic beverages), limit the hours of operation, and require the casinos to send monthly statements to all rewards card or "comp card" club members. Bill Kearney is real smart and street savvy. He knows he doesn't have much of a chance of getting any of these safeguards approved, with the possible exception of the monthly statements.

Kearney argues that since casinos use reward cards to track their customers' wins and losses and reward them for time spent gambling (and money lost) by giving them complimentary meals, rooms, and merchandise, they should also send them monthly statements, just like credit card companies do. That way, consumers can keep track of their spending habits or, rather, their wins and losses. Drawing on his first-hand experiences of being treated like a VIP and given all kinds of free perks as long as he was spending—and losing— hundreds of thousands of dollars in Atlantic City casinos, Kearney calls comp cards the casino addict's syringe. "This is how they [the casinos] deliver their drug. These cards track every move the patron makes in the casino. This determines whether you're going to get the buffet or the penthouse suite. The comps or so-called freebies make some [people] justify their losses as they become addicted."

Bill Kearney is right about the comps in terms of their use as tracking devices. I was surprised when I finally understood what the cords connecting people to slot machines were all about. How can people be so gullible? With the money they let the slot machines suck up, they can go out and buy most of what's offered as comps or rewards. More important, why let the casinos have so much information about you, everything from your age to where you live and work to how much you're giving them each time you visit? Casinos don't have to work hard to keep track of the outrageous profits they earn each month. Much of that work is done by the rewards card club members each time they stick their card in a machine.

I remember once visiting Jack Binion's Horseshoe Casino in Hammond, Indiana. After getting over my embarrassment and shame of seeing a commercial I'd done several years earlier playing nonstop on the flat-screen monitors that were hanging everywhere, I was a bit flabbergasted when a woman sitting at a slot machine next to me boasted about being a member of the casino's VIP club. She proudly showed me her VIP Members card and said that she regularly eats at the VIP buffet and gets all kinds of other perks, like valet parking. I wondered how much it cost her in losses to boast about her VIP casino status, but of course, I didn't ask.

As I watched the videos on YouTube that Bill Kearney forwarded to me after our meeting in December of 2006, I was surprised at the opposition to his proposal for monthly statements. Just about everyone, from Pennsylvania governor Ed Rendell on down, argued that safeguards already are in place to "mitigate harm" to consumers while maximizing gambling revenues. They dismissed Kearney's insistence that existing safeguards, such as counseling services and twenty-four-hour gambling addiction help lines financed by the casinos, are after the fact, after the consumer has become "a casino-gambling degenerate," as he claims he once was.

Kearney asks policy makers, "Why wait until someone gets addicted? Let's make our billion-dollar gaming operators who are already tracking their patrons' gaming activities adapt to a real safeguard, and that is to mail out monthly statements that will enable gamblers and their family members to address a loved one's gambling problem before it gets out of hand."

The casino industry doesn't want consumers to start thinking about how they're spending their money. Casinos can't turn enormous profits if people start rationalizing their expenditures or budgeting their visits and wagers, which many of them did during the economic crisis of 2008 and 2009.

◆ ◆ ◆

After I returned to Detroit and settled in to spend New Year's Eve with my father, I asked him about the casinos and black people's reaction to them. He told me what I already knew: the casinos are bad for this economically strapped city. "A lot of people are straining to win and they're losing. They can't pay their bills. As I read the papers, I see a lot of them going to jail because they're embezzling money and it's all because of those damned casinos."

Early in the afternoon on New Year's Eve, I asked my father to take a ride with me. I told him I wanted to go on a tour of the city, to the places where we once lived. We started out on the North End and stopped in front of the house on Cardoni where he and Momma raised their first four children. The neighborhood looks desolate. The few remaining houses are rundown. Trash-filled vacant lots are everywhere. A block away, on Cameron, a neighborhood development project had put up a few new houses here and there amid the urban decay. I shuddered to think about the families who would move into them and how vigilant they would have to be to keep their children safe.

Daddy described the new houses and the squalor around them as checkerboard pockets in the city where impoverished sections of a neighborhood or block are adjacent to areas that are neat and well maintained. The problem is that urban decay, the result of city cutbacks in services such as garbage collection, has taken over the areas that are trying to make a comeback.

Everywhere I looked as we drove around the neighborhoods where I once lived, I saw trash in vacant lots. The lots are dumping grounds for old furniture, mattresses, and garbage and hadn't been cleared in months, a result of then-mayor Kwame M. Kilpatrick's efforts to balance the city's budget without increasing property taxes. To be sure, many other factors contributed to the city's dire straits, the most significant being the collapse of the auto industry, which sent the unemployment rate soaring above the national average.

In an April, 2006 address to the Detroit City Council, Mayor Kilpatrick ticked off all the things he'd done over the past four years to balance the budget. Although he presented them as accomplishments, they were hardly worth celebrating. He *cut* some of the city's essential services, such as rubbish removal, and laid off more than 5500 city employees, including police officers and fire fighters. The city employees who remained were required to take a one-year, 10% pay cut and risked seeing reductions in their health care and pension plans.

Nowhere were the effects of these cuts more evident than in the steadily decreasing city population and in neighborhoods where uncollected rubbish are breeding grounds for rats. People are leaving the city for employment elsewhere in ever increasing numbers. Those who remain must contend with having their property overrun with rubbish. Mayor Kilpatrick discussed the problem of trash collection in his address. "No issue has received more attention in recent weeks than the issue of trash collection. In the current fiscal year we eliminated monthly, curbside bulk trash pickup in the City of Detroit, saving approximately $20 million for our general fund the equivalent of about 250 police officers. I made that choice in the belief that most Detroiters would rather eliminate bulk pickup than lay off an additional 250 police officers."

Therein lies the rub. Wagering taxes from the casinos were supposed to help pay for some of the services that were being reduced or eliminated by Mayor Kilpatrick. According to an e-mail I received on June 18, 2007, from Eric T. Bush, the Administrative Manager of the Detroit Gaming Control Board, in 2006 Detroit casinos took in more than $1.3 billion and paid $155 million in revenue taxes to the City of Detroit's General fund which "can be spent on almost anything." (Casinos in Detroit took in more than $1.2 billion in 2009). But, what was the money being spent on? The Gaming Board's web site states, "The City's portion (11.9% of the casinos' Net Win) may be used by the City for the hiring, training, and deployment of street patrol officers; neighborhood and downtown economic development programs designed to create local jobs; public safety programs such as emergency medical services, fire department programs, and street lighting; anti-gang and youth development programs; other programs that are designed to contribute to the improvement of the quality of life in the City; relief to the taxpayers of the City from one or more taxes or fees imposed by the City; the costs of capital improvements; and road repairs and improvements."

Instead of offering relief, the city imposed more fees. Detroit residents are now required to pay $25 per month per household to help finance trash collection. Qualifying senior citizens receive a 30% reduction in the fee, but that might not be enough for impoverished senior citizens who are already stretched to the limit. Since Kilpatrick didn't want to raise property taxes, the fee is added to the property tax bill and must be paid at tax time. But it's not a tax; it's a fee payable to the City, or so the Honorable Mayor told his citizens.

◆◆◆

My father and I drove along Oakland Avenue, which runs through what was once the North End's thriving black business district. The shops, bars, and businesses began closing during the mid-1960s; the 1967 riot finished them off. Like everywhere else we visited, the area is marred by abandoned houses and buildings and trash-filled vacant lots. Its one great glimmer of hope is the work that former Detroit Pistons basketball star and NBA Hall of Fame member Dave Bing is doing to try to revitalize it. (In May of 2009, Bing was elected to serve out the term of Kwame Kilpatrick, who was forced to resign after being found guilty of perjury and sent to jail. Bing was elected to a four year term as Mayor on November 3, 2009). As founder and chairman of the Bing Group and chairman of the Next Detroit Neighborhood Initiative, Dave Bing not only is trying to keep manufacturing jobs in the city; he's trying to clean up North End neighborhoods by bringing down the old, abandoned, and burned-out houses and putting up new and affordable single-family dwellings.

Bing also launched a $60-million project to develop condominiums on an old industrial stretch of the Detroit riverfront with the hope of attracting more affluent buyers back to the city. It's a gamble, a risk Bing feels compelled to take in order to help bring the city he adopted long ago, when he was the Pistons' star player, back to life. He acknowledges that the condominiums will be too expensive for many Detroit residents, but he also knows that solid middle-class communities such as the one he's developing are vital to the city's rebirth. He told a reporter for *The Houston Chronicle,* "If you want to bring communities back, some decisions have to be made. You can't forget about poor people, but you have to have a middle class. You just can't have a city full of poor people." He hopes that his project will entice some of the professional people who work downtown to live there rather than in the suburbs.

Before heading home to Strathmoor Street from our New Year's Eve tour of Detroit, my father and I drove to the East Side and stopped at the corner of Holcomb and Forest. "Why're we stopping here?" Daddy asked. "Because I used to live on this street, right over there." I pointed to a brand new single family house, one of three now standing in the spot where Gloria and I and our children watched the 1967 riot. The old buildings were demolished a few years ago. These new houses were just completed; three pretty new houses standing amid weed-infested and litter-filled vacant lots waiting for their proud new owners to move their families in.

I pointed to one of the houses and said, "I lived in a big old wood frame building, in a rear apartment right where that new house is. That's where I was when the riot happened." I turned to look at my father. "Daddy, you never came to visit me here. You never once came to visit me in any of the dumps where I used to live." He looked out his window. He didn't say anything, but I could tell he didn't want to talk about it. Why churn up unhappy memories in a man who's nearly a century old?

We drove downtown to his former place of employment, the Patton Parking Garage. The building was still there; the deep blue sign still hanging on the building's façade. (It has since been demolished). We parked in front of the office. Sitting there looking through the large plate glass window, I had a happy memory, as if it had happened yesterday, of going there with my mother to meet my father and sitting quietly in the little lobby with my brother Jimmy and my sisters, waiting for our sweet-smelling daddy to take us on a joy ride up and down the ramps.

As we headed home Daddy said, "This drive was an eye-opening experience for me, because I've not been in the areas we saw today in years. I haven't been downtown in years because there's no reason for me to go downtown. Ain't nothin' there except those casinos."

Later in the evening, as we settled in to await the New Year, Daddy brought out all the family photo albums. One had newspaper clippings he'd saved from the 1943 race riots. Yellow and faded and crumbling, they include photos of black people being pulled off trolleys and beaten and white mobs chasing and beating black women and men as they tried to make their way out of a downtown movie theater to safety. They made my stomach churn. The articles and photos are ugly reminders of the racism that lay simmering in the city's social structures after 1943, only to flare up again with devastating effects in the summer of 1967.

Among the family photos was one of my mother in the kitchen. Two babies—my oldest daughter and my little brother John—were playing on the floor under the table where my mother was busy preparing a meal. The date stamped on the photo was 1962. Where was I? In the Juvenile Detention Center? I had much I wanted to say to my father that day and later that night, when we were alone celebrating New Year's Eve. I wanted to say that I was sorry for the pain I caused him and my mother. Sitting with him that night and looking at family photos wasn't easy, though. I couldn't help but think about my mother and how much she loved my father and how he betrayed her over and over again. I kept it all to myself. Just try and enjoy this time with your father, I told myself. That six-day visit was the longest I'd spent with him in more than twenty-five years.

◆◆◆

Since I had to go back to Madison before January 13, when my father planned to celebrate his ninety-first birthday at MotorCity Casino, we went there shortly after New Year's Day to check it out. Daddy said he was amazed at how packed the place was with black folks gambling. It was around 1:30 in the afternoon when we arrived. As we walked around the casino, he kept muttering, "What're all these people doing up in here? Don't they work? With the economy so bad, where're they getting the money from to gamble?"

Good questions. I could understand it if had been New Year's Eve or New Year's Day, but this was Thursday, January 4, 2007, a workday for most people. How many of these people were out of work? How deeply were they in debt? All this was running through my mind as we walked around looking at the people entertaining themselves. I found it ironic that the murals and paintings decorating the casino's lobby walls depicted men hard at work on assembly lines building cars, reminding patrons who take the time to look that this city was once the motor capital of the world.

After we walked around the MotorCity Casino for a while, Daddy settled for a ten-times-pay quarter machine. I gave him $50 and went my way. I found a butterfly machine. I fed it a twenty-dollar bill and it rewarded me with $200, exactly what I had brought with me. I had almost doubled my "investment." "Okay, that's enough," I told myself. "I'm just here to check this place out, to see for myself what black folks in this city are doing with their money."

By the time I made my way back to where my father was sitting, I had lost all the money, almost $400. It took about thirty minutes. Daddy was having better luck. His single credit plays were hitting; he was satisfied. After about an hour of watching his credits go up and down, he was ready to go.

That trip to the casino was a big adventure for my father. He loves to talk, and this gave him something new to talk about. By the time my sister Carla came home, Daddy was in high gear, going on and on about his experience. Some of what he said was funny, especially when he started talking about all the old people he saw, as if he's not beating the hell out of a century of living on the planet.

He told Carla, "I have to say, I was amazed about how many old-assed people were in that place. Old people everywhere. In wheelchairs, on canes. It's not the Lord's house. We passed the Lord's house on the way there. There's a church on every corner in this city, and most of them people needed to have their old asses there, on their knees praying, instead of gambling. It's not that I'm against old people. Hell, I'm old my damn self."

Daddy explained the new ticket in–cash out redemption machines the casino had recently installed so people don't have to stand in line at the cashier's desk to redeem their vouchers. "You put your ticket in. The machine sucks it up and kicks out some money. At first I didn't know how to use it, but a lady came by and helped me. You know, everybody thinks because I'm old, I need help. I don't need no damn help, I just needed to know how to get my money without standing in a long line."

The thing that struck him the most, aside from the number of elderly people in the casino, was the look of desperation many of them wore on their faces, a scene I had witnessed far too many times. Daddy shook his head in disbelief as he talked. "I saw an old lady just laying on the machines, stretched out across three machines, trying to play them all at the same time. A man was walking around with an oxygen tank. These people looked like they were about to die. What is this? With the economy like it is, where are all these old people—they got a foot in the grave!—where are they getting the money to let the casinos suck it up like this?"

At one point in his ramblings I reminded my father that he wasn't doing anything different from the other old folks.

"Daddy, some of those people are doing what you did. Didn't you tell me you used to go because you got bored sitting in the house? That's why they go to the casinos, because they're bored or lonely. They're looking for something to do, some place to go where they feel welcome."

"Yeah, but the difference is, I got a strategy."

"Okay, Pops. What's your strategy?"

"My strategy is this. I never bring more than a hundred dollars. And once I get to a machine, I stay there. I rarely ever change machines. I feel this way, either I'm gonna get the machine or it's gonna get me. I see no reason to go running around looking for another one. They're programmed to give out so much. For me, going to the casino isn't about the money anyway. I go there for myself, to relax. I prefer to go by myself and be alone. I don't like to take other people because they might lose what they got, and if you're winning, they want to borrow some money. If I'm alone I can meditate while I'm sitting at the machine, until the $100 runs out. A hundred dollars will let me stay at the casino two hours, and that's enough. When the $100 is gone, I'm gone. And that money doesn't affect my budget."

I started to remind him that he was behind in his property taxes, but I wasn't supposed to know that. Brenda snooped around in his room one day and found the notice about the property taxes and called me and told me about it. We were worried. Here he was, talking about how he can afford to lose $100, and that's only at the casinos. He spends $17 a week on lottery tickets, but he doesn't consider that gambling.

I don't mean to suggest that my father has a gambling problem. As far as I can tell, he doesn't spend much time running to casinos, and he sends a neighbor to the local liquor store to buy his lottery tickets. At his age he doesn't have the energy for much else. My point is simply that my father is a perfect example of how gambling takes advantage of the most vulnerable and financially unstable members of inner-city black communities.

My father has a theory about gambling: "My theory is that this is a gambling establishment. They're in business to make money, not give it away. And when I go, I like to sit near the stage where I can see the girl singing while I'm playing the machines."

"What girl, Daddy?"

"Whatever girl they got singing."

"Oh."

"There used to be a big white girl with red hair singing. You know, she had a bluesy sound. If she was there singing, then I was just fine to sit there and put my few dollars into the machine. But I was not about to lose everything I came in with, no siree. A hundred dollars. That was the most I'd allow myself."

"Well, Daddy, like I said, you're doing the same thing those other old people are doing. Next time you go, on your birthday, ask some of them. If they bother to talk to you, they'll tell you they also have a theory and a winning strategy. And be sure to let the customer services people know it's your ninety-first birthday so they can announce it and give you a gift, like a clock or some other piece of junk you don't need. That's what they gave Carla for her birthday. A cheap clock with the MotorCity logo on it that was made in China and probably cost them about fifty cents. Or less. Of course she had to go to the casino to pick it up. Can you image that? A place that doesn't even have clocks, gives out cheap clocks for birthday presents! They send you a card and tell you to come and get your present."

It suddenly occurred to me why my father wanted to go to MotorCity Casino on his birthday.

"Daddy, did they send you a birthday card telling you to come and get your present? Is that why you want to go on your birthday? Do you have one of those rewards cards?"

"Yeah," he said. "I got that card around here somewhere. I'm supposed to bring it with me."

He went into his bedroom and started rummaging through the stacks of papers on his dresser, pretending not to hear me. My father has a bad habit of claiming he can't hear when he wants to tune people out. I followed him into the bedroom and turned up the volume.

"Daddy, that's how they hook people."

"What's that, daughter? What's that you say?"

"Daddy, you heard me. The casino industry ain't stupid. Those cards and cheap gifts are nothing but marketing gimmicks. That's the way they lure you in, so you can drop some money. They know they've got a big market in old people. Why else would the Greektown Casino use an image of Rosa Parks to lure people in?"

A few months earlier I'd read an article in the *New York Times* recounting how Rosa Parks's image was being used to market all kinds of things, like the Chevy Silverado and Greektown Casino. I thought to myself, "Detroit has hit an all-time low. Nothing is sacred or revered, not even images of Rosa Parks if they can help bring in the bucks." The ad, showing a smiling Rosa Parks alongside the phrase, "What a Ride," ran in the *Detroit Free Press* shortly after her death in 2005.

I was in a food co-op with Mrs. Parks for almost a year in the late 1970s and sometimes saw her on Saturday mornings when she came to get her groceries. I chatted with her often enough on those days to know damn well that she wouldn't have wanted her picture used to promote gambling. Or anything else, for that matter.

The question I began asking myself after I read the article was "What about me?" I don't mean to imply that I'm some kind of national heroine, but Rosa Parks had no say in how her image was used. She was dead. I have choices. I'm not so desperate an on-camera actor and commercial print model that I can't say no to an ad campaign that promotes something I've come to believe is detrimental to the well-being of many of this nation's citizens. Yet in April of 2007, I responded to a call from my Chicago talent agent to audition for a television commercial for the Illinois Lottery. I made the first cut, got a callback, and a week later was booked for the job.

My agent called and congratulated me and said, "Oh, by the way, they're going to want to put a rinse in your hair to cover the gray. I'm just telling you this so you won't freak out." My agent knows me well. I have a thing about my hair. I don't use chemicals or dyes and I like my silver curls. They're very much a part of who I am. Also, after having lived in Madison, Wisconsin, for twenty years, I've endured more than my share of white beauticians and hair stylists apologizing that they can't give me an appointment for a haircut because their shop doesn't do "ethnic hair," whatever that means. I agreed to the coloring because my agent assured me that "*they* were going to do it," which I interpreted to mean that the clients were providing the stylist.

On the day of my wardrobe fitting, I looked in a mirror and told my reflection, "They're going to see how pretty this hair is and forget all about the gray." They didn't. After we finished with the wardrobe selections, one of the ad agency's assistants called me back into the conference room where about fifteen people—directors, members of the creative team, and representatives for the client, the Illinois Lottery—were gathered. One of the women, a white woman, said to me, "We want you to get your hair colored to cover the gray." I asked a couple of questions about dyes and rinses and said, "Okay. So who's going to do it?" She said, "We want you to go and get it done, and we'll reimburse you."

That's when I hit the ceiling. I'd already spent much of the morning running around downtown Chicago trying to find a pair of athletic shoes without a logo, one of many wardrobe items I was asked to bring. Now they wanted me to put myself through what for me is an ordeal to satisfy whatever idea they had of what I should look like. I told them that this is natural hair, that I don't want my hair colored at all, and since they want it done, they ought to hire somebody to do it instead of asking me to go through a lot of stress and trauma.

To put it bluntly, I freaked out. I had a major meltdown in front of a roomful of high-powered advertising executives and directors. They finally agreed to send me to a hairstylist in Chicago who works with black peoples' hair. I think they just said that to get me out of the room. No sooner was I in my car to drive back to Madison than my agent called on my cell phone and informed me that I was being dropped from the shoot; I had been fired for being "very difficult" about my hair. I shouted at my agent, "It's precisely because it's my hair that I'm being difficult! The Illinois Lottery spends millions of dollars a year on advertising, but these agency people are too cheap to bring a hairstylist onto the set who knows how to work with this black woman's brand of 'ethnic hair' and I'm not about to go running around to find somebody to do it. I don't want my hair colored! They do, so they ought to take care of it."

It took me about a week to get over this bad hair day. Not only had I been fired from a job that just about every commercial actor in Chicago wanted; I had strained my relationship with my agent. But this wasn't just about my hair.

When I look back on this experience, I have to admit that, given what I know and have experienced about gambling, I should never have agreed to audition for the Illinois Lottery commercial in the first place. That's what was at the bottom of this episode. I'm sure that's what was going on in my muddled thinking. Deep down inside of me was a conflict about my choices. Here I was, in the process of writing a book that takes a critical look at casino gambling. I was struggling with my own compulsive gambling, yet I had agreed to help promote the very thing, albeit in a different form, that I was intellectually opposed to.

It's not like this job was going to make a big difference in my annual income. I make a good salary as a senior professor. I'm by no means wealthy, but I have everything I need to live a comfortable life. As long as I stay out of casinos, I'll remain financially secure. I don't need to be an accomplice to this high-tech fleecing of my father and millions of other poor black people like him.

◆ ◆ ◆

I left Detroit the day after my father and I went on our MotorCity gambling adventure. Driving along I-90 near Elgin, Illinois, I passed a billboard advertising the Grand Victoria Casino. I had every intention of continuing straight ahead to Madison. Instead, I took the I-25 exit and went to the Grand Victoria. I lost $500.

CHAPTER 11

The Abyss

Sunday, February 4, 2007, 1:30 a.m.

It comes in spurts, these urges to go to casinos and play the slots. What happened tonight was downright scary. I'm lucky to be alive.

◆ ◆ ◆

Every time I thought I had a grip on my bad gambling habit, it gripped me. This time it was a stranglehold. I'd finally achieved something I'd been working toward for years. The Penumbra Theatre in St. Paul, Minnesota, had cast me in a play, *Blue,* a comedy by Charles Randolph-Wright.

Penumbra is one of the most prestigious black theater companies in the country. It's where the Pulitzer and Tony Award-winning playwright August Wilson made his professional debut—and where most of his plays had their premiere under the direction of Lou Bellamy, the theater's founder and artistic director. Being cast in a show by Lou Bellamy is an important artistic accomplishment, as far as I'm concerned, especially since I started so late in life and have no professional training beyond the intensive workshops at Shakespeare & Company. It was all coming together—the teaching, writing, acting. So why was I trying to blow it all by bankrupting myself? Or killing myself?

That night in February of 2007, I did something so frightening I couldn't sleep. On my way back to Madison from St. Paul, I stopped at the Majestic Pines Casino in Black River Falls. The previous week I'd gotten lucky at Ho Chunk on my way home and won $1,000. As I was folding my $100 bills into my coat pocket, I'd sworn to myself that I wasn't going to try this again. I was spending Sunday nights in Madison so I could teach my classes on Mondays, then I'd head back to St. Paul and stay the rest of the week. I was an "artist-in-residence" at Penumbra Theatre. It sounded nice, but it was a lot of driving, about four and a half hours each way. But it was so worth it.

The problem was that I had to get past the billboards that beckoned me to the Majestic Pines, which is about halfway between Madison and St. Paul, and only four miles east of the interstate. And I literally drove right past Ho Chunk Casino when I turned off the interstate onto Highway 12, which took me into Madison. Anyway, I decided to try my luck again, even though the few times I'd been to the Majestic Pines, I found it even more depressing than the other Wisconsin casinos I visited. All those old people roaming around looking nervous and disappointed because the slots weren't paying out.

It was Superbowl Sunday, 2007. The slot machines were eerily quiet. Not many people were there. Everywhere you looked, televisions were blaring the results of the game. Every now and then a slot player would stop hitting the Bet Max button to see who was winning. The employees stood around looking bored out of their minds. I started with $200. I lost that quickly, then did something I'd sworn I wouldn't do again. After exceeding the daily allowable limit for ATM withdrawals, I started writing checks.

The woman at the cashier's desk told me that Ho Chunk casinos have a new system. Now you have to leave your thumbprint on your checks. I asked her if she would like a saliva swab, too. "You know, a little DNA?" She didn't crack a smile. "No," she said, "Your thumbprint will do." It didn't occur to me to ask why she needed my thumbprint—I assumed it was one more piece of information the gambling industry was gathering about its guests, patrons, suckers (take your pick). Two hours after I entered the Majestic Pines, I'd lost $1,500.

My intention was to go straight home. It was getting late and I was tired. Instead, I drove right to Ho Chunk, parked my car, ripped a blank check from my checkbook, and strode inside, determined to win some of my money back. The lady at the cashier's counter took the check I'd written out for $500 and my thumbprint and informed me that I'd reached my limit.

"My limit for what?" I asked.

"You have a $1,000 limit. You can only write checks for up to $1,000 within an eight-day period. That's your limit."

I asked her to explain.

"Well, it takes about eight days for the checks to clear, so we put on limits. You cashed a check for $500 up at Majestic Pines, so now you've reached your limit. In eight days, after these checks clear, you can write up to your $1,000 limit again."

I thanked the cashier for the information and started trying to grind out some money from the slot machines. I got lucky again—three triple stars symbols fell on the payline of a Superstars Spin machine. The bonus reel sped around. I held my breath as it landed between two bonus symbols that would've more than doubled my win. I walked away from the machine with $1,180. I cashed my voucher in, tucked the hundreds away, and played $80 on the Wild Cherry machine. It spat out $200. Now I had $1,300. I didn't break even, but at least I got some of the money back. It was time to leave.

If only that triple stars machine's bonus reel had landed on the ten-times-pay symbol. I would've won ten grand. Damn!

I was tired. On my way home I was doing seventy miles per hour and blanked out, just for a second, long enough to end up in a ditch. Luckily there weren't any other cars out there. I wasn't hurt, and the car wasn't damaged. Lucky for me.

Up until that near-disastrous Superbowl Sunday, I'd sustained myself whenever I went into a casino by invoking the voice of Dennis Krausnick, my acting teacher from Shakespeare & Company. Sometimes I felt as if he were standing next to me, coaching me in his soft voice. "Don't lose yourself, Sandy. Stay connected to your text and you'll be okay."

He was talking about all the emotion—the anger and rage—that was wrung out of me each time I went for an intensive acting training workshop. "Allow yourself to feel the emotion, but stay in the moment, Sandy," he'd say, noting that my character—Queen Margaret—was very angry and intent on revenge for the murders of her husband and son. "Allow yourself to feel that anger and speak your text!"

At some point I'd begun to think of the casino as a performance space and myself as a performer. The experience was similar to stepping onstage and entering the world of whatever play I was in, except that I was not connected to those around me. I was not in the moment. The me that was in the casino was someone else, this woman I'm writing about. Sandra Adell doesn't gamble. I felt like I was outside myself, peering into a looking glass, observing and recording myself and others from somewhere else.

As the gambling experiences became more intense, I lost the voice that kept urging me to stay connected to my text. I could no longer hear Dennis. I could no longer see the face of Barbara Hermansen staring at me from the page of *Chicago* magazine that had been sitting on my desk for more than a year to remind me where I was headed. I kept telling myself that I was not a gambler, that I was there to collect the material that would become this book. In the interest of my writing I had to take this as far as it could go; I had to let the experience run its course.

Almost exactly two years after it began, it ended on May 31, 2007, the night I lost myself and my text. The slot machines had sucked the me right out of me.

◆ ◆ ◆

It started out as a beautiful Friday evening. I was excited; I was going to learn something new. I had just joined the University of Wisconsin's Equestrian Club and was going to take my first horseback riding class. As I started out to the stables in Belleville, Wisconsin, the instructor called to say that the lesson had been canceled. It had been storming off and on all day out there, and they weren't letting the horses out.

I was disappointed, so I went to the Union Terrace, a popular gathering place overlooking Lake Mendota where people come to eat brats, drink beer and wine, listen to live music, and watch novice sailors and windsurfers trying to stay upright and afloat. I bought a glass of chardonnay, sat on a balcony with an overhang that protected me from the rain, and watched the storm pass over the lake. On the way home I bought a bottle of chardonnay and spent the evening sipping wine and watching *Law & Order*. Then a commercial for Ho Chunk popped up on my television set, showing happy people playing slot machines "where the winners are."

Suddenly, I just knew I would win if I went to where the winners are. I'd been drinking, but that didn't stop me. According to my receipt from a nearby ATM, at 9:38 p.m. I withdrew $200 from my checking account and left Madison for Ho Chunk.

I don't remember how long I stayed or how many bottles of Heineken I drank while I was there. I remember becoming very agitated as I moved from one machine to the next, trying to find the jackpot. I finally cashed in my vouchers, put three hundred-dollar bills in my pants pocket, and left with several twenty-dollar bills in my hand. It was very late. I was a few steps from my car when something shiny on the ground caught my attention. It was a woman's watch. I bent down to pick it up.

The next thing I remember, I was surrounded by the casino's security guards. There was quite a bit of commotion. One guard was talking on a cell phone; another one was helping me up off the ground and asking me to pick up my money. "Pick up your money, ma'am." I remember standing there, looking at the money and wondering why all these men were around me. The watch was in my hand. "Ma'am, pick up your money, and give me your car keys. You've had too much to drink. We can't let you get behind the wheel. Give me your car keys. You can get them when you've sobered up."

I obeyed. I picked up my money and got into the backseat of my car. They locked me in. I went to sleep. I woke up several hours later and went back into the casino to get my keys. A customer services representative called a security guard. His name is Orlando. I asked him what had happened. I admitted that I was drunk, but why were some many people around me? Orlando said, "Someone came into the casino and reported that a woman was lying on the ground in the parking lot. You had passed out a few feet from your car."

"What? I passed out?" I felt my head. It was sore; there was a bruise on the left side of my forehead.

"Yes. You had too much to drink. We couldn't let you drive. We helped you off the ground and asked you to pick up your money. You just stood there looking at it, as if you didn't care about it."

I told Orlando that I didn't care about the money; I cared about what was happening to me. I told him about my book and admitted that this was as far as I could go. I'd had enough. He asked me if I wanted to exclude myself and explained how it works.

"We photograph you, have you sign papers banning yourself, and if you show up on any of our properties, we can have you arrested for trespassing."

That's what Barbara Hermansen did at the Grand Victoria Casino. It didn't stop her from gambling. She just went to Indiana and kept right on playing the slots. I thanked Orlando and told him that I would immediately seek counseling. I had had enough. I had fallen into the abyss. I didn't need to kill myself. This had all become too unreal.

The next week I went into intensive therapy. It took months for the anxiety induced by two years of gambling to subside enough for my therapist and I to begin dealing with the more than forty years of unresolved issues that had somehow brought me repeatedly to the casino floor. I'm still dealing with them, trying to unravel whatever it was that set me on such a disastrous path. I still don't know why this happened, although a 2001 study on gambling and addictions conducted by Dr. Hans Breiter and his colleagues at Massachusetts General Hospital provides a disturbing explanation. They compared scans of the brain of a cocaine addict receiving a dose of cocaine and scans of the healthy brain of a control subject who was playing a game of chance in a laboratory setting.

The result was astonishing. Breiter told a documentary film maker for Casino Free Massachusetts, a nonpartisan coalition fighting the introduction of casino gambling in Massachusetts, "You looked at the activation of the primary rewards system in the center of the human brain, when they were a cocaine addict expecting a cocaine infusion, out [sic] versus a normal control expecting a monetary win. We saw the same thing. They were nearly identical. And I could not distinguish who had received cocaine versus who had won a gambling task." Even with this kind of scientific evidence about the effects of gambling on the brain practically at my fingertips, I remained in denial about my addiction, although many things continued to trigger in me powerful urges to gamble, like the sound of my laptop booting up, certain cell-phone ringtones, radio and television commercials inviting us to "Win! Win! Win!", and the sight of hundred-dollar bills.

After staying away from casinos for more than a year, I relapsed on July 10, 2009. Earlier that week, I cashed a check for $300 and asked to be paid in hundred-dollar bills. Whether or not the bills were the trigger, I can't say. Alcohol certainly was a factor; I'd been drinking heavily off and on for several months. That evening, I decided to drink some wine, just one bottle of chardonnay. I didn't stop there. After I finished the bottle, I walked to the wine shop and bought another. I drank it. The next thing I remember, I was being arrested on Highway 12, the road leading to Ho Chunk Casino. I was handcuffed, placed in a police car, taken to the Sauk County Jail, and booked for drunk driving.

The last thing I remember about that night was thinking that I had come full circle, except that now I was not a frightened, four-teen-year-old pregnant teenager. I knew better. As a jail guard locked me in a cell, I said to her, "This is almost just like the one I was in when I was a kid, except it didn't have a concrete cot. It had a metal cot. I think I'll write about this. I'm a writer, you know."

I was released the next day. I immediately placed myself in intensive outpatient therapy for alcohol and drug abuse. I'm still in therapy. I still ask the same questions: "Why did this happen? Why did I *let* this happen?"

◆◆◆

In my house in Madison, a woman's silver watch lies on the kitchen counter where I can see it every morning as I make my cappuccino. That watch saved my life. In my mind, I see myself being hand-cuffed and placed in the back seat of a police car. The state trooper who arrested me saved my life. The glass face on the silver watch is broken; its hands point at 1:30. My time is up.

EPILOGUE

As my journey through the Labyrinth comes to an end, it remains somewhat unreal to me. I know I survived because of the one resource that has sustained me throughout my life—my high level of literacy. I love to read. Sometimes I think I've lived too much in books, too much in my mind. But that's where I'm most comfortable, where I'm most at home.

Among my favorite writers is the Russian novelist Fyodor Dostoevsky. In February of 2000, while visiting St. Petersburg, Russia, I went to the last of the corner flats he lived in while he worked on his masterpieces and gambled away his money as quickly as he earned it.

It was not a happy visit, my trip to Russia. I had taken a train there from Finland, where I had led a dissertation defense for a Finnish student who wrote his thesis on the African American novelist, Richard Wright. The student's faculty committee had identified me as an "expert" on Wright and his literary relationship with Russia's most famous novelist, Fyodor Dostoevsky. In fact, Wright's novels had introduced me, long ago, to Dostoevsky.

While standing in the apartment at 5/2 Kuznechny Pereukok and listening to a docent speaking in Russian about Dostoevsky, tears began slowly seeping from my eyes. I quickly and discreetly wiped them away. I didn't question my strong emotional reaction to the memory of this man who is so far removed from me historically, geographically, culturally, racially. I often respond emotionally to writers whom I've come to love. I recall standing in the little memorial museum, not understanding a word of what was being said and thinking about his novel, *The Gambler*. It was published in 1866 and remains one of the most provocative narratives of gambling and loss ever written.

Set in the fictional German town of Roulettenberg, the novel is filled with unscrupulous, greedy, and hopelessly deluded characters who prey upon each other as they struggle with their obsessions and their increasing financial debts. The novel's protagonist, Alexey Ivanovitch, tutors children in a family that is awaiting the death of its wealthy matriarch, Antonida Vassilyevna Tarasyevitchev, so family members can receive an inheritance. Although her relatives have been notified by telegrams of her impending demise, Granny, as she is called, makes a surprise visit to Roulettenberg and loses a fortune at the casino's roulette tables, with Alexey at her side.

Alexey's description of Granny's frenzied behavior—and later his own as he too gambles and wins and then loses a fortune—is not unlike the behavior of twenty-first century slot players: "Granny could scarcely sit still in her seat. She stared with feverish eyes at the little ball dancing on the spokes of the turning wheel. . . . Granny was beside herself, she could not sit still, she even thumped on the table with her fist when the croupier announced, *"trente-six"* instead of the *zéro* she was expecting. 'There, look at it,' said Granny angrily, 'isn't that cursed little *zéro* coming soon? As sure as I'm alive, I'll sit here till *zéro* does come."

The seventy-year-old Russian landowner loses everything she brought with her to Roulettenberg but not everything she owns. She still has her land. Alexey is not so lucky. He gambles at the table; he gambles with his love, first for Polina Alexandrovna and then the avaricious Mlle. Blanche. And he loses.

Dostoevsky wrote *The Gambler,* his most autobiographical novel, in twenty-six days. He had made a very bad deal with his publisher for an advance of three thousand rubles, which he desperately needed to pay his expenses and gambling debts, and risked losing the rights to all his published work if he didn't deliver this manuscript by

November 1, 1866. Dostoevsky turned the completed manuscript in just hours before the deadline.

As I stood in his apartment, I wondered what it was like for this great writer to be so caught up in gambling and debt that he had to write quickly to stay out of debtors' prison. How does one will the kind of creative imagination it takes to write so quickly and so profoundly about the human spirit?

I attributed my sadness to my solitude. I felt it more intensely in St. Petersburg than ever before, the result of being by myself in a country where I didn't know anyone and couldn't understand, speak, or read the language. For four days I talked to no one as I made my way to the monuments and museums in this place that I knew only through fiction, through the novels and stories of Fyodor Dostoevsky.

Today, as I finish my text, I wonder whether what I experienced there that day was what people often refer to as spiritual—a connection across space and time with Dostoevsky for reasons that would not become clear to me for eight years.

I began this book in a desperate effort to try to understand why this thing was happening to me. Now that the slots have released their hold on me, I'm playing with a fantasy—that Dostoevsky spoke to me that day when I went to his apartment in St. Petersburg. It's only now that I can translate what he said. He whispered to me as I stood there. "Remember *The Gambler*," he said. "Let my story be a cautionary tale."

November 16, 2009
Madison, Wisconsin

ACKNOWLEDGMENTS

I am grateful for the support and encouragement I received from many people as I underwent this journey into the labyrinth.

I thank my colleagues in the Department of Afro-American Studies at the University of Wisconsin-Madison: Tracy Curtis, Christina Greene, Freida High W. Tesfagiorgis, Michael Thornton, Craig Werner.

I thank the scholars and anti-gambling activists whose work inspired me to continue writing even as I was losing control: Anita Bedell, Diane Berlin, Renee Cunningham-Williams, Tim Falkiner, Reverend Tom Grey, Earl Grinols, Bill Kearney, John Kindt, Gerda Reith, Don Weinbaum.

Many thanks to the great people who put me all back together again: Laura Menningen, Kristina Nilsson, Jennifer Parker, Monroe Whitlock.

Thanks to Melba Joyce Boyd, Jon Gramling, David Robertson, Mary Tufts, Rachel Volberg, Kathy Wildfong, and John Wright for taking time out of their busy schedules to read and comment on drafts of the manuscript.

I am very grateful for my friends and family—my children and grandchildren, my father and brothers and sisters, especially my sister Brenda, to whom I dedicate this book.

ABOUT THE AUTHOR

Sandra Adell is a literature professor, actor and commercial print model. She teaches in the Department of Afro-American Studies at the University of Wisconsin-Madison. A native of Detroit, she has lived in Madison for more than twenty years.